THE FLASH OF BRILLIANCE WORKBOOK

The Eight Keys to Discover, Unlock, & Fulfill Your Creative Potential at Work

Other Titles by William C. Miller

Flash of Brilliance: Inspiring Creativity Where You Work

The Creative Edge: Fostering Innovation Where You Work

n the island of Crete, at the edge of the open sea, mighty King Minos engaged the master architect and proud craftsman, Daedalus, to build an impenetrable labyrinth to imprison the ferocious Minotaur. Daedalus worked tirelessly to erect the massive stone maze as his son Icarus sat nearby and watched with wonder. When it was finished, Daedalus ushered in the tethered and deadly beast, and unchained it so it might roam within the labyrinth walls.

Daedalus boasted to King Minos that his creation was so strong and so clever that neither human nor beast could ever escape it. So the king put the labyrinth to its ultimate test. He locked Daedalus and Icarus up in the maze with the deadly Minotaur. Trapped in his own creation, Daedalus spent many days outwitting the vicious beast as he searched for a way to escape. At last he found his way to freedom. With bravery and cunning, he worked feverishly at the lock, and freed himself and his young son from the death-maze of the Minotaur.

Daedalus and Icarus fled to the rocky caves on the other side of the island, and pondered their destiny. "King Minos rules the land and the sea. We cannot escape that way," said Daedalus, as he watched the seagulls flapping their wings and gliding through the air. "But he does not rule the skies." And so he set out to fashion shining wings of feathers and wax that could lift them up into the air and to their freedom.

Then one windswept morning when the wings were complete, Daedalus and Icarus fastened them onto their shoulders. Daedalus warned his son not to stray too close to the blazing sun, and then the two flapped their arms like the birds and rose to ride the skies off the island. Their hearts soared with their flight as they headed towards Sicily. But young and foolish Icarus couldn't resist temptation as he rose higher and higher in the air. The hot sun soon melted his wings and he fell to his death in the sea, leaving his father to journey alone to Sicily.

When Daedalus reached Sicily he was welcomed warmly into the court of King Cocalus. He was invited to remain on the island to serve the king's subjects and to continue his life's work. And it was there on Sicily where the master craftsman, now filled with respect and humility, built his offering to the god of the sun, the glorious temple of Apollo.

Daedulus' mythic journey is a metaphor for the one we all take when we explore our creative potential. Daedalus faced two creative challenges. First, he had to escape from the labyrinth, a symbol for old patterns of thought and belief that trap us. Second, he had to find a creative way to leave the island, to resolve a worldly challenge. Daedalus matured by the end, using his creativity less to serve his pride and more to serve his community.

WILLIAM C. MILLER
WITH JANICE LAWRENCE

THE FLASH OF BRILLIANCE WORKBOOK

The Eight Keys to Discover, Unlock, & Fulfill Your Creative Potential at Work

PERSEUS BOOKS
Cambridge, Massachusetts

Perseus Books is a member of the Perseus Books Group

Book Design: Diane Dias, Mill Valley, CA
Typography: Futura, Times, Marydale, and Envision

1 2 3 4 5 6 7 8 9 10- -0201009998
First printing, December 1999

Perseus Books are available at special discounts for bulk purchases in the U.S. by corporations, institutions, and other organizations. For more information, please contact the Special Markets Department at HarperCollins Publishers, 10 East 53rd Street, New York, NY 10022, or call 212-207-7528.

Find us on the World Wide Web at
http://www.perseusbooks.com

This book
is dedicated to the
divine creativity
in every person,
every day.

Table of Contents

"Man is what he believes."

■ Anton Chekov

You are a unique person, with your own special blend of talents and personal values. Every day you face a series of challenges that invite you to use your talents and values to make a difference. When you do, you are being creative!

Your personal creativity is your ability to use your thoughts, values, emotions, and actions to enrich your environment and yourself in new and unique ways. It's more than just a clever mind! And this program is much, much more than just "creative thinking skills."

Creativity will help you take on new challenges in your life. You'll feel more self-confident and work better with others on problems. You'll develop more creative options and find solutions that reflect your personal values. You'll put your ideas into action and celebrate your success.

Recognize Your Creative Potential

To increase your creative power you need to do three things.

- Recognize your creative potential.
- Develop the skills you need to exercise your potential.
- Choose to use your creativity every day.

And that is just what this program will help you to do.

You may not be sure you want or need to be more creative. Or you may not believe you really could be if you wanted to. That's OK. This program is designed to help you to recognize your own potential and your own reasons for developing your creativity.

So, Whose Ideas Are These Anyway?

This approach was developed by William C. Miller, Principal Consultant with the Global Creativity Corporation, an organization dedicated to helping individuals and entire organizations develop strategic approaches to innovation.

Mr. Miller is a recognized authority on personal creativity and fostering innovation in the work place. He is the author of *The Creative Edge: Fostering Innovation Where You Work* and *Flash of Brilliance: Inspiring Creativity Where You Work.*

Formerly, Mr. Miller was the head of the Innovation Management Program at SRI International and Director of Training and Development for the Victor Equipment Company.

This program is based on Mr. Miller's experience working with more than one hundred major U.S. and multinational corporations. Additionally, he conducted four major studies of creativity and innovation in industry. They included:

- direct interviews with Fortune 500 company executives who had the responsibility for integrating innovative, entrepreneurial firms into their company.
- an analysis of databases that correlated how differences in American values and lifestyles are reflected in how people chose to express their personal creativity.
- a synthesis of academic research, corporate studies, and general literature on creativity produced over the past forty years.
- an original study of the Innovation Styles of hundreds of working people in a wide range of corporate jobs.

Why Is Completing This Book So Important to You?

The more that stresses compound your life and your work, the more you need to be creative… and the more you need to inspire everyone around you to exercise their creative talent as well. The quality programs of the last decade proved that every employee has the potential to contribute creative ideas.

What do you want to do, and contribute, with your limited time on earth? We are by nature creative engines, running twenty-four hours per day. What do we do with this creative power? Many of us let it idle, or we power up without consciously knowing where we want to head.

What's the alternative? It is to navigate your life with a clear sense of personal values as your compass. We all have goals in life, from taking care of our family to having a certain career, but what is the thread of continuity — the purpose — that runs through these goals and gives them unity and continuity?

You can state your purpose in six different ways. There may be some overlap in your answers, but start from the top of this page and work down through the questions on page 4:

KEY QUESTION AND EXAMPLES	YOUR OWN ANSWERS
What possessions or social status do I wish to acquire? *I want a comfortable retirement with a home in the Caribbean; I want to be a respected leader in my church.*	
What milestones do I wish to achieve? *I want to be part of growing this business by 25 percent each year over the next five years.*	
What type of experiences do I wish to have? *I want to work with people of different cultures from all seven continents.*	

KEY QUESTION AND EXAMPLES	YOUR OWN ANSWERS
What gifts and talents do I wish to make to others? *I want to provide my children and the people who work with me the best opportunity to fulfill their career aspirations.*	
What difference do I wish to make to others? *I want to provide my children and the people who work with me the best opportunity to fulfill their career aspirations.*	
What type of person do I wish to become? *I want to become an everyday example of a person who is loving, trustworthy, and truthful.*	

As you can see, your purpose becomes more and more basic to your soul as you move to increasing depth.

Examine honestly all your key ambitions and activities at work, and see which statement(s) you find most enduring across all of them. That's the basis of your real-time, not-just-nice-sounding, personal purpose.

Your personal purpose is the driving force for expanding and investing your creativity, where the payoff for you is greater meaning, satisfaction, even enthusiasm and fun. The payoff for others is the benefit of the unique difference only you can make in their lives.

"Work is love made visible. When you work with love, you bind yourself to yourself, and to one another, and to God."[2]

■ Kahlil Gibran

Your search for personal purpose and meaning must ultimately go beyond how you acquire things and experiences to a deeper, more resonant meaning. You can find this meaning amidst the creative expression of your mind, heart, and soul. With a tremendous amount of courage — literally, "heartfulness" — and you may have to lead the way to a new story about success in business.

In light of your personal purpose, what are your goals for completing this workbook? Think and feel at a deeper level than just, "I want to become more creative" or "I want ways to solve the problems in the XYZ project." What do you want to get out of it?

What would make this work on creativity most meaningful to you?

Describe what you want to accomplish be completing this workbook, in words and a symbol. (Go ahead and draw something. Take a risk.)

"Precisely because you are aware of the limits of life, you are compelled to bring forth what is within you; this is the only time you have to show yourself. You can't waste away in a meaningless job, cramming your life with trivia. The supreme insistence of life is that you enter the adventure of creating yourself."[1]

■ Brian Swimme

What This Book Is About

The *Flash of Brilliance Workbook* is designed to help you develop your creative potential at work or at home.

What Can It Do for You?

Look in the mirror. This book will help you gain a better understanding of your personal creative power. You'll learn about how you like to exercise your creativity.

Take a daily dose. This book will help broaden your horizons about when to apply your creativity. It will sharpen your awareness of the many different opportunities for creative expression you come across every day.

Build your strength. This book will help you develop the eight creative skills that are the keys to becoming a master of the creative process.

Listen to your heart. This book will show you how to harness the power of your values in order to keep yourself motivated in the face of risk and uncertainty.

Take a guided tour. This book will help you make your creative ideas happen. It will take you on a personal creative journey and guide you every step of the way.

Who Is This Book For?

Project managers
Crane operators
Your girlfriend
Doctors
Computer hacks
Astronauts
Receptionists
Accountants
Research chemists
Actors
Bankers
The boy next door
Pharmacists
Homemakers
Sales managers
Auditors
Shopkeepers
Cabbies
Great Aunt Alice
Plant managers
Reporters
Your dad
Mechanics
Graphic designers
Your daughter
Singers
Bakers
Candlestick makers...
(or anyone else who is interested in kicking up their heels and making their life more exciting)

"I cannot teach anybody anything. I can only make them think."

■ Socrates

"A first-rate soup is more creative than a second-rate painting."

■ Abraham Maslow

Personal Creativity is the ability to use your thoughts, values, emotions, and actions to enrich your environment in new and unique ways. You can express your creativity every day. The way you dress, how you organize your work, or your special recipe for five-alarm chili are all products of your unique creativity.

But, do you recognize when you are using your creativity?

You may not feel that your job requires you to be creative. Your responsibility may be to carry out the orders, not make them up. After all, what is so creative about figuring out a way to smooth out the peaks and valleys of the work flow, or planning an off-site meeting that is both fun and productive, or cracking the right joke that helps your boss laugh her way through a tough day?

Well believe it or not, these situations are also ways for you to exercise your unique creative spirit.

There Are Many Different Ways to Express Your Creativity

Everyone recognizes famous artists and inventors as being creative. But have you ever thought about all the creativity it took to come up with the things we use every day?

Produce an Event

People had been thanking the gods with harvest feasts for thousands of years before the Pilgrims decided to celebrate the first American Thanksgiving. But it was the bright idea of a Pawtuxet Indian named Squanto to use the celebration as a way to solidify the friendship between the early English settlers and the Native Americans.

Producing an event is a great opportunity to exercise your personal creativity. Whether you are throwing a birthday party for your six-year old or a retirement banquet for the Chairman of the Board, an event invites you to think imaginatively about what you are trying to accomplish and how to do it in a memorable way.

Express Yourself Artistically

Storytelling is one of Man's oldest traditions; myths and stories were how our ancestors explained the inexplicable. But who came up with the idea to tell fairy tales? Many of the stories we read to our children before they fall asleep, like *Cinderella* or *Sleeping Beauty*, were first written down by Charles Perrault, a Frenchman who made his living by telling stories at the court of Louis XIV.

Music, art, and poetry are all products of our desire to create. From time to time we all find ourselves making up stories, singing songs, dancing at a disco, or drawing sketches of how we want to rearrange the living room furniture. If you think about it, you probably create a work of art every day just to make your life more interesting and enjoyable.

Think Up a New Idea

The world may remember Leonardo da Vinci for Mona Lisa's smile, but the fact remains that he was the first person to come up with the idea for contact lenses. Way back in the 1500's, he figured out the best way to correct poor vision was to put a "short, water-filled tube sealed at the end with a flat lens" against the eye. Since then millions of dollars have been spent perfecting this idea, and it's just in the past few years that we have finally developed the technology to make Leonardo's idea work.

Coming up with new ideas or improving on old ones is a common way we focus our personal creativity. What is surprising, however, is how many new ideas are needed every day. Whether you are looking for new ways to market your product, refinance your home, or a cure for cancer, the ability to generate ideas is the key to your success.

Make Something Tangible

"If nobody else is going to invent a dishwashing machine, I'll do it myself." Josephine Cochrane of Shelbyville, Illinois made this proclamation in 1886 and proceeded to go out into her backyard and build the first dishwashing machine. Although her first model was crude compared to today's standards, she gets the credit for inventing a major kitchen appliance.

Inventing and building tangible objects is another application of our creativity. Sewing a dress, building a cabinet, or making a Valentine are all ways that you may be applying your personal creativity already.

Do Something Spontaneous

The next time you are sitting on the beach enjoying the cool taste of an ice cream cone, think about who came up with this bright idea. In 1904 an ice cream vendor named Arnold Fornachou at the St. Louis World's Fair ran out of paper dishes. Fortunately, his stand was right next to a Syrian baker who was selling zalabias, a thin Persian waffle. Legend has it that Fornachou bought a waffle, twisted it into a cone, scooped in some ice cream and a great treat was born.

Acting in a spontaneous way is another outlet for our personal creativity. Using your wit to spice up the dinner conversation, making up a new game to entertain your son, or figuring out a quick and easy way to settle a dispute are all examples of how you spontaneously generate new and unique ways to deal with everyday situations.

Organize People or Projects

While serving as a British soldier in the Boer War, Colonel Robert Baden-Powell became concerned that young men from England lacked the strength of character and resourcefulness required to inherit the responsibilities of managing the British Empire. So he decided to form a club for boys that would imbue them with the attributes of loyalty, courage, and leadership. This club, founded in 1908, has grown to be the Scouting Movement that provides education and direction for boys and girls all over the world.

Organizing people or projects is another common outlet for our personal creativity. Whether you are reorganizing your closet or your multinational corporation, you need to call upon your creativity to figure out the best way to do it.

Build a Relationship

In 1530 the famous Dutch philosopher and educator, Erasmus, came up with the bright idea that children should learn manners. In order to spread the word he wrote the treatise, *On Civility in Children,* which was responsible for developing western culture's traditions for the education of young children.

How you build relationships with others is another way you manifest your creativity every day. Whether you are setting the standard for professional behavior in your advertising agency or working on improving the communications between you and your dad, figuring out how to deal with other people constantly challenges your creativity.

Change Your "Inner" Self

Jean Nidetich was fat. She tried out lots of fad diets that didn't work. She was frustrated. But in the early seventies she figured out the best way to lose weight and keep it off was to change her attitude towards herself and food. She just decided that "Nothing tastes as good as being thin feels," and the key idea behind Weight Watcher's Inc. was born.

Weight Watcher's Inc. is a group that has helped thousands of people lose weight by helping them develop a new belief about themselves. Being open to new approaches to how we live our lives and think about ourselves is another way we can use our creativity to make our lives richer and more fulfilled.

How do you use your creativity every day? Think of an example of how you used your creativity to come up with a unique way to:

- *Produce an event*
- *Express yourself artistically*
- *Think up a new idea*
- *Make something tangible*
- *Do something spontaneous*
- *Organize people or projects*
- *Build a relationship*
- *Change your "inner" self*

Creative People Have Eight Skills

You may feel more creative at some times than at others. How can you tap into your creative potential more often? Does your "muse" visit you just by chance?

No.

A synthesis of research about creativity in many different cultures reveals eight creative skills. By practicing these skills you can develop your ability to use your creativity effectively and readily. Mastering these skills will help you become more successful in meeting the challenges you face in new and unique ways.

This workbook will help you develop those creative skills. Some of them you might already have mastered. Others, you may need to develop. Let's start by taking a personal assessment of your past experience in applying these skills.

1. ***Read over the chart.***
2. ***For each skill, think about when you have applied the skill to help you take a new or unique approach to meeting a challenge.***
3. ***Note the situations and how you applied the skill.***
4. ***Note what happened to you as a result of using the skill in your situation.***
5. ***Note how you felt when you applied the skill to your situation.***

AS A CREATIVE PERSON, YOU ARE ABLE TO:

See the big picture

When you look at a sand bar and "see" the next Miami Beach.

Take initiative

When you decide you are going to do something about the mess in the plant by organizing a Safety Task Force.

Be open to new ways of doing things

When you decide to hold your staff meeting off-site, even though it's not in the budget.

Look for input from others

When you ask your sales managers to participate in your ad agency's brainstorming session.

Generate many options

When you help your twins make their Halloween costumes.

Make decisions based on your values

When you decide to assign the account to the new kid in order to help her grow.

Take action and be persistent

When you organize fifty dinner parties to raise money for the new wing of the hospital.

Share the credit and reward yourself and others

When you throw a surprise party for your wife to celebrate her graduation from medical school.

When did I use this skill in the past?	How did I apply the skill?	What happened as a result of using the skill?	How did I feel when I used this skill?

As you read this section, evaluate yourself on your abilities by checking the appropriate box.

See the Big Picture

"The future belongs to those who believe in the beauty of their dreams."

■ Eleanor Roosevelt

So often it is the dreamers who make the difference. Creative people are able to see the big picture when everyone else is mired in the details. They have a clear idea of what they want to accomplish. And they have the ability to express their vision so others can join them in their quest.

This workbook will help you improve your ability to see the big picture by showing how your values can motivate you to broaden your horizons, and encourage you to go out and take on a challenge. You'll find yourself saying something like:

I make a difference!

- ☐ *I'm good at this already.*
- ☐ *I want to develop this skill.*

Take Initiative

"In the middle of difficulty lies opportunity."

■ Albert Einstein

For the creative person a "risky" situation is a challenge. Even in the face of adversity, they are stimulated by the chance to make things better. They don't let the "status quo" or a fear of failure stop them before they start. They take the initiative to find the silver lining in every cloud.

There can be many stumbling blocks that get in the way of you pursuing your creative dreams. This workbook will help you become more aware of what these blocks are and provide you with strategies for overcoming them. You'll find yourself saying something like:

I am stimulated by uncertainty and challenge!

- ☐ *I'm good at this already.*
- ☐ *I want to develop this skill.*

Be Open to New Ways of Doing Things

"Let's not look backward in anger or forward in fear, but around in awareness."

■ James Thurber

Often the greatest, single barrier to coming up with new ideas is a desire to hold on to old ones. To maximize your creative potential you need to have the self-confidence to be flexible in your outlook and be open to trying out new ways of doing things.

In this workbook you will learn about the importance of being open to new ideas. You'll discover that by not judging new ideas right away, you give them the time they need to develop into something special. You'll find yourself saying something like:

I am confident and creative!

- ☐ *I'm good at this already.*
- ☐ *I want to develop this skill.*

Look for Input from Others

"It is better to know some of the questions, than all of the answers."

■ Mark Twain

Creative people know they don't have all the answers. Since they recognize the creative potential in everyone, they don't let organizational structures or prejudice limit their creative exploration. They search out other people's ideas and welcome diverse viewpoints. They want others to challenge their ideas because they know it will make them better.

This workbook will help you take a more democratic approach to developing new ideas. You'll master the tools and develop the attitudes you need to invite others to contribute to your creative efforts. You'll find yourself saying something like:

I welcome diverse viewpoints!

- ☐ *I'm good at this already.*
- ☐ *I want to develop this skill.*

Generate Many Options

"Nothing is more dangerous than an idea, when it is the only one you have."

■ Emile Chartier

It takes a lot of ideas to come up with a good one. Successful creative people are able to generate many options. They know about and use many different idea-generation techniques. Some are analytical and exercise the mind; some are intuitive and exercise the heart.

This workbook will help you become more inventive by teaching you many new ways to generate lots of ideas. You'll find yourself saying something like:

I search for options with my heart and mind.

- ☐ *I'm good at this already.*
- ☐ *I want to develop this skill.*

Make Decisions Based on Your Values

"Be sure you are right and then go ahead."

■ Davy Crockett

Creative decisions are the toughest to make. Often there are no "facts" and "figures" to prove that this idea is the best way to go — just a feeling that you know in your heart this is the right thing to do. Creative people are evaluative; they are capable of seeing both sides of a situation and making a decision based on their personal values.

This workbook will improve your ability to make creative decisions by encouraging you to respect what is most important to you when it comes time to make a choice. You'll find yourself saying something like:

I decide based on my values!

- ☐ *I'm good at this already.*
- ☐ *I want to develop this skill.*

Take Action and Be Persistent

"Our greatest glory is not in never falling, but in rising every time we fall."

■ Confucius

Perseverance is the key to making your novel ideas work. Once you have figured out what to do, you need the courage to take action and the stamina to champion your idea through thick and thin.

In this workbook you'll figure out how to sell your idea to others and build the support network of people and resources you'll need to implement your idea successfully. You'll find yourself saying something like:

I persevere through thick and thin!

- ☐ *I'm good at this already.*
- ☐ *I want to develop this skill.*

Share the Credit and Reward Yourself and Others

"The reward of a thing well done is to have done it."

■ Ralph Waldo Emerson

Creative people love their work. They can't imagine doing anything else, because what they do is so exciting. This attitude toward life is so satisfying they are free to share their success with others. They give credit where credit is due and encourage others to join them in celebrating their accomplishments.

In this workbook you will learn about the many different sources of creative satisfaction to help you become better at recognizing success and rewarding others and yourself. You'll find yourself saying something like:

I am thankful for our success!

- ☐ *I'm good at this already.*
- ☐ *I want to develop this skill.*

T I P

For more information about the applications and skills of creativity, refer to Chapters 1, 2, & 7 of *Flash of Brilliance: Inspiring Creativity Where You Work.*

Creative Inspiration Comes from the Heart

When you're committed to achieving a goal that is important to you personally, you look for every way possible to make it happen. That's your creativity at work; that's when you are working at your best.

What inspires you to give your very best?

Each of us has our own special reason for putting the extra effort into our work. Our desire to make a difference is fueled by our personal values — our need for well-being and peace, our sense of responsibility and truth, and our very human need to love and care for others.

What does it take to really live and work by your values?

Understanding how to apply your values to your work is a critical step to unleashing your creative power. You can take a creative approach to any situation, but if you spend your creative energy on unimportant tasks, eventually, you'll "burn out." However, if you choose to apply your creative power to challenges that are important to you, you'll find yourself energized.

The following quotes summarize what motivated them to do a creative job.

Service

"We are all given gifts of creativity to be used in service to other people; which is also a way to serve ourselves. I was very excited about this unique opportunity to come over to the U.S. and teach Americans about Japanese management systems, in return for the fact that we Japanese have imported so many ideas from the U.S.

Creativity is just the means of carrying out the basic opportunities given to us. You can always 'waste' your talent creating gadgets. But I'm talking about creativity in the service of affirming life. And the more you use it the happier you become."

■ Seijun Yanagida, Trainer in Cross-Cultural Communications
New United Motors Manufacturing, Inc.

Well-being

"I think it is wanting to help people — it's helping on the outside, and on the inside, too. Because when you put together a diverse team and try to awaken the creativity that probably hasn't been utilized for a number for years, it helps them. It really changes what they are about; it's a kind of inside and outside well-being."

■ Sue Gatchell, Director of Product Concept Development
General Motors Corporation

Responsibility

"In the lumber mill this summer, I saw people who weren't really giving very much of what they could. And I knew there was so much more just waiting to be unleashed. I'm excited about helping find ways to help them realize that potential. When we eliminate fear, it empowers people to achieve what they want to; what they feel they need to. What really turns me on is what we say in the employee involvement program ... that we want to celebrate the infinite potential of the individual."

■ Barbara Hinca, Project Coordinator for Operations Improvement
Simpson Lumber Company

Creativity

"It's always fun to be creative ... I have found the most fun about creativity is the experience itself, whether or not the outcome is what you expected or wanted. The biggest leaps ... the more fun ones ... come from taking two radically different ideas and making a very simple, easy to understand, 'I-wish-I-had-thought-of-that' idea."

■ Gerry Pierce, Director of Electronic Technology
SRI, International

"The height of your accomplishment will equal the depth of your convictions."

■ William R. Scolavino

Truth

"I hung tough on not accepting business that we couldn't deliver on. That was a test. I would talk to a customer, look him in the eye and say, 'Do you want me to lie to you?' I used words that had an emotional impact, but there was no ambiguity ... they accepted that. It turned out that we could execute good business, deliver on that business, and manage it to a schedule, even though there were threats of going someplace else or walking away from it."

■ Dick Eppel, General Manager

Quality

"Quality today is possibly an overworked word, but the type of work that I'm proud of is a bit uncompromising. Oftentimes, it's really no more time consuming to do it right — to exercise care and understanding of the implications of your design ... an appreciation of the hidden messages of quality."

■ John Gooden, Vice President of Marketing and Design
Design West, Inc.

Communication

"I have been trying to improve the relationship between the company, and the employees and their unions. Just to get them to understand each other so they can solve their common problems together is a major undertaking. I honor both cultures being represented. Their joint success is what matters to me.

One way is getting them to talk about, 'What do I want individually, and as a representative of my organization, to result from this day?' I help them hear from each other the very powerful areas of common interest we could pursue, that would be good for both unions and the company."

■ Roger James, Organizational Development Consultant

Peace

"The problems are surely there. The work is never done. We don't look just at the problems, we look at the possibilities. That really does make a difference. Successful experience builds the confidence. That's probably grown over time."

■ Mary Nelson, President
Bethel New Life, a community development corporation

Love

"We produced the customer seminar on a shoestring budget with not very much time. We pulled off something entirely miraculous. It takes a lot of love and care for what you're doing. It takes a lot of passion. It takes a lot of belief that your product is going to bring value to someone else. It took a lot of love and care in the quality of our work ... We care about our customers. That's why we're in the field. That's why we're salespeople."

■ Dana Soo Hoo, Account Representative
Pacific Bell

Excellence

"We talk about empowering people to realize personal excellence and achievement by expanding their abilities to make profit-making changes and quality improvements. When I say that, I'm also talking about myself. I'm constantly wanting to be on the growing edge, finding the new things going on in the world that are making things better, and then finding a way to bring those into the corporation or community."

■ Paul Everett, Director of Operations Improvement
Simpson Lumber Company

Great Results Grow Out of Putting Your Most Fundamental Values to Work.

Your values are a great source of energy; energy you will need to pursue your creative adventures.

What values inspire you to do your best work?

Service: the importance of contributing to the welfare of others.

Well-being: the importance of having respect for others' happiness and quality of life.

Communication: the importance of openly listening and sharing information, thoughts or feelings.

Peace of Mind: the importance of being in a state of harmony, calm, and self-confidence.

Creativity: the importance of expressing your uniqueness and taking new approaches for continual improvement in your work.

Responsibility: the importance of being accountable for the results of your actions.

Quality: the importance of putting full worth, reliability and personal commitment into work.

Truth: the importance of honesty and integrity in your thoughts, words, and deeds.

Excellence: the importance of putting service, communication, creativity, and quality into everything you do.

Love: the importance of caring to bring well-being, peace, responsibility, and truth into your own and others' lives.

"Keep peace with the drummer you hear, however measured or far away."

■ Henry David Thoreau

TIP

Review your personal purpose from pages 3-4. See what values are embodied in your purpose.

"Success is a journey not a destination."

■ Ben Sweetland

You may be lucky enough to stumble across a great, new idea at the perfect moment which materializes into a revolutionary, new product that makes you a million dollars. But the odds are that you will win the lottery first.

Good ideas only become great ones when they are molded and shaped into useful, practical solutions that solve problems and meet needs. This isn't always easy. It takes a lot of effort, courage, and creativity.

There is a process, however, to guide us along the path to practical solutions.

Whether we are an entire country trying to put a man on the moon or a manager turning around an ailing company, our creative endeavors tend to share a common process.

A process is a series of actions that lead to a particular result. A process gives you a road map to follow and a structure to work within.

Understanding the creative process helps you become more effective when you are applying your creativity. You'll plan better, become more aware of the potential problems, and anticipate what it really takes to reach your goals.

But there is more to rising to meet a challenge than just following a series of steps. Exercising your creativity is exciting and stimulating. Exploring the world of the unique and unknown can be a grand adventure. To reflect this kind of challenge we shall refer to the creative process as a Creative Journey.

The Creative Journey Has Four Distinct Phases:

- **The Challenge** — when you decide on what you want to accomplish despite the risks in your path.
- **The Focus** — when you define your problem or opportunity.
- **The Solution** — when you generate ideas and find your solution.
- **The Completion** — when you implement your solution and use your experience to find your next challenge.

TIP

One of the most wonderful things about the Creative Journey, is that it is chock full of surprises. You never quite know what will happen next. You may find that your Creative Journey doesn't always happen in a smooth, predictable, step-by-step way. So feel free to jump ahead in the process, but do yourself a favor and don't skip any of the steps completely.

The Challenge

STEP 1

Discover Purpose

The first step of the process is to identify and verbalize your general purpose or goal. Develop a vision of what you want to accomplish and understand what motivates you to take on this challenge.

STEP 2

Assess Risks

The next step is to recognize and deal with the uncertainty of trying something new in this situation. Take the initiative to accept whatever risks or obstacles come your way, and make the personal commitment to overcome them.

The Focus

STEP 3

Know Yourself

The next step is to look inside and get in touch with your self-confidence so you can use it as a source of strength when the journey becomes difficult. Be more receptive and accepting of new ideas.

STEP 4

Analyze Priorities

Now that you have taken on the challenge, it is time for you to define exactly the problem that you want to solve or the opportunity you want to develop. Seek out other people's ideas and concerns, so you can be sure that you focus on the right situation.

The Solution

STEP 5

Develop Options

The next step is to generate as many ideas as possible that could contribute to your solution. Using both your intuitive and analytical mind, and how you feel in your heart, helps you be as inventive as possible.

STEP 6

Make Decisions

Whether your idea is as momentous as the discovery of relativity or as simple as a new way to clean the ring out of the bathtub, the moment of breakthrough only comes after you have sifted through many ideas. Choose the best solution based on what is important to you.

The Completion

STEP 7

Implement Plans

Each step of the implementation will be a little victory for your idea. Persevere against all odds and be flexible enough to change or adapt your solution to meet the needs of the real world.

STEP 8

Celebrate Results

It is important to recognize your success and to enjoy it. Take the time to celebrate your results and you'll find new energy and enthusiasm for your next challenge.

TIP

The Creative Journey is never-ending. Once you have met one challenge, you will be eager to start the next one. Reexamine your creative experience and see how it has changed your values and aspirations.

Your Creative Past

One of the easiest ways to understand how the Creative Journey works is to apply it to a real life example. This exercise will help you understand what your past creative experiences had in common.

1. ***Think back to a challenging situation you faced either in your personal or work life.***

   The kind of situation would have been one in which:

   - *You had to deal with new problems for the first time.*
   - *You really cared about resolving the problem successfully.*
   - *You had to come up with new solutions and try out ideas that you hadn't used before.*

   Examples of this kind of situation might have been:

   - *Launching a new product.*
   - *Balancing a new baby with the demands of your work life.*
   - *Taking care of a parent who had a sudden and serious illness.*
   - *Starting in a new sales territory.*

2. ***Describe your situation by answering these nine questions. Express yourself in pictures and/or words.***

What was the initial goal of your creative challenge?

What uncertainty did you face — what made it a tough challenge?

What was it about yourself (your values and character) that helped you keep going when the going got tough?

How did you define the real problem?

What ideas and options did you come up with?

What was your "breakthrough" solution?

How did you implement your solution?

How did you assess and celebrate the results?

What new goal did you want to accomplish next?

No One Ever Said that Doing Something New for the First Time Was Going to Be Easy...

As you embark on your Creative Journey, you may feel overwhelmed by the enormity of your challenge. Or you may find that your energy and enthusiasm wane as you have to deal with one obstacle to your progress after another. Further on, you might find that people don't want to accept your new ideas or participate in their implementation. And you may feel let down once the project is over.

On the other hand, even if you come up against these potential stumbling blocks, you don't have to let them slow you down. Your skills, values, and enthusiasm will carry you through.

A Creative Journey is bound to be an emotional one. Accept the fact that there are going to be ups and downs. One way to overcome the blocks that might get in your way is to anticipate them up front. Some blocks are internal — you get in your own way — and some blocks are external — others get in your way. Learn how to deal with both kinds of blocks.

This exercise will help you evaluate what kinds of blocks have gotten in your way before and give you some ideas of how to get around them.

Check off the internal and external blocks that you have come up against in the past.

"Who cares?"

Apathy is usually what keeps you from getting started on a creative project. You just find life boring or nothing seems important enough to require putting out any extra effort.

- ☐ *I've said this to myself.*
- ☐ *Others have said this to me.*

"Don't rock the boat!"

Sometimes you are just too comfortable with the status quo to be bothered by trying to change or improve the situation.

- ☐ *I've said this to myself.*
- ☐ *Others have said this to me.*

"What if I fail?"

Fear of failure is a sure show-stopper. If you feel like you are going to have to solve this problem all by yourself or that you aren't going to get any help from anyone else, it is easy to feel overwhelmed by the challenge and discouraged from moving ahead.

- ☐ *I've said this to myself.*
- ☐ *Others have said this to me.*

"No wonder I can't solve the problem, I don't even know what it is!"

Problems and opportunities are funny things: they often come disguised as their symptoms. If you are unable to define the real problem, you may end up wasting a lot of time and energy.

- ☐ *I've said this to myself.*
- ☐ *Others have said this to me.*

"I have the perfect idea ..."

Once you think you have the perfect idea, it is time to try to generate a whole lot more. Judging ideas too soon limits your ability to imagine any more. It also discourages you from using others to help you.

- ☐ *I've said this to myself.*
- ☐ *Others have said this to me.*

"It will never fly at corporate."

Compromising ideas before they have a chance to work or setting too many limits on which ideas might be accepted is a great way to keep you from ever finding a breakthrough to an exciting and novel solution.

- ☐ *I've said this to myself.*
- ☐ *Others have said this to me.*

"Do it my way or die."

Just because the implementation is your responsibility, it doesn't mean you can't learn from and listen to others. And if you don't involve others you may find they won't give you the support you need to get the job done.

- ☐ *I've said this to myself.*
- ☐ *Others have said this to me.*

"Big deal ... it worked ... all in a day's work."

It is important to recognize a job well done. If you are always rushing on to the next job, eventually you will "burn out." Take the time to celebrate the victories.

- ☐ *I've said this to myself.*
- ☐ *Others have said this to me.*

"You'll never amount to much."

■ Munich schoolmaster's evaluation of ten-year old Albert Einstein.

"You don't have any creative, original ideas."

■ Midwestern newspaper publisher's feedback to young Walt Disney.

"Your voice sounds like wind whistling through a window."

■ Enrico Caruso's first voice teacher.

"We don't like their sound. Groups of guitars are on their way out."

■ Decca Recording Company's reason for turning down the Beatles in 1962.

"Master Einstein, you will never amount to much."

Nothing is more frustrating than being excited about a new idea and finding yourself surrounded by nay-sayers and cynics.

Take heart. Even the most indefatigable optimists have their moments when they begin to lose their positive outlook. Take a lesson from these famous "failures." They changed things despite the odds. How did they do it?

Successful innovators use their personal sense of values and creative curiosity to focus their energies and keep themselves motivated in the face of adversity.

As you get ready to start a Creative Journey, you can probably count on getting stuck more than once. Each step of the journey has a few blocks that can get in your way. Some of them may slow you down for a while and others may not faze you at all. If you do find yourself lagging in enthusiasm, however, stop for a minute and think about **why** you're doing what you are doing.

Although each one of us has a unique reason for every creative challenge we undertake, research has shown that certain values are great energizers at the various steps of The Creative Journey. And while your reasons may differ from ours, try using ours as a guideline for your Creative Journey and see what you learn.

The Challenge

STEP 1

Discover Purpose

When you are trying to get started on a new creative project, you may encounter an atmosphere of apathy. Try thinking about your commitment to service — imagine how your project has the potential to really contribute to the welfare and happiness of others or yourself. Remind yourself:

I make a difference!

STEP 2

Assess Risks

Once you have made a commitment to taking on a creative challenge, you may come up against the "status quo." If you are feeling complacent, take a hard look at your and others' future well-being. Insuring a bright and secure future will inspire you to make positive changes. Remind yourself:

I am stimulated by uncertainty and challenge!

The Focus

STEP 3

Know Yourself

As you progress in your Creative Journey, you are going to reach a crisis point where you just don't know if you're going to succeed. Stop, look inward, and re-establish your peace of mind and self-confidence about your project. This will help you to be more flexible and open-minded. Remind yourself:

I am confident and creative!

STEP 4

Analyze Priorities

When you start to search for your solution, everyone will have a different opinion of what you need to do. This can be very frustrating. To make it through these trying times, remember the value of communication. Welcome diverse viewpoints. Gather all of the information you need to be sure that you engage the right situation. Remind yourself:

I welcome diverse viewpoints!

The Solution

STEP 5

Develop Options

When you are developing options you need to be as inventive as possible. If you find that your ability to generate lots of solutions gets bogged down, remind yourself that you are trying to come up with a creative solution; one that is truly unique and has not been done before. Remind yourself:

I search for solutions with my mind and heart!

STEP 6

Make Decisions

Sometimes, it's easy to compromise too soon or put off making your decision. If you are about to settle on a less innovative solution in the interest of making it "acceptable," tap into your sense of responsibility. This is your project and you are accountable for its outcome. Make your decision based on your personal values and you will be more committed to seeing it succeed. Remind yourself:

I decide based on my values!

The Completion

STEP 7

Implement Plans

Making your idea work in the real world can be the toughest part of the Creative Journey. You may not get the support you need right away; it may take years of sweat to realize your dream. Make a commitment to quality. Your creative idea is unique and deserves to be implemented in the best way possible. Remind yourself:

I persevere through thick and thin!

STEP 8

Celebrate Results

You've made it. You have finally seen your dream come true. Have you stopped to recognize your and your collaborators' accomplishments? Take the time to look at the truth of what you have achieved. What have you accomplished? What have you learned in the process? Share this truth with others and give yourselves a pat on the back. Remind yourself:

I am thankful for our success!

Setting Your Creative Goal

Take the time to answer the following questions. They will help you find opportunities to exercise your creative muscle.

1. Recognize your creative potential; how would you like to focus your creativity?

- ☐ *Produce an event.*
- ☐ *Do something spontaneous.*
- ☐ *Express yourself artistically.*
- ☐ *Organize people or projects.*
- ☐ *Think up a new idea.*
- ☐ *Build a relationship.*
- ☐ *Make something tangible.*
- ☐ *Change your "inner" self.*

2. Can you think of a situation in the near future that would give you an opportunity to do so?

1. Which creative skills would you like to develop?

- ☐ *See the big picture.*
- ☐ *Generate many options.*
- ☐ *Take initiative.*
- ☐ *Make decisions based on your values.*
- ☐ *Be open to new ways of doing things.*
- ☐ *Take action and be persistent.*
- ☐ *Look for input from others.*
- ☐ *Share the credit and reward yourself and others.*

2. Can you think of a situation in the near future that would give you an opportunity to do so?

1. ***What personal values are motivating you to develop your creative potential?***

- ☐ *Service*
- ☐ *Responsibility*
- ☐ *Well-being*
- ☐ *Quality*
- ☐ *Peace*
- ☐ *Truth*
- ☐ *Communication*
- ☐ *Excellence*
- ☐ *Creativity*
- ☐ *Love*

2. ***Can you think of a situation that would give you an opportunity to put these values to work?***

1. ***Who would you like to involve to help you grow and develop your personal creativity?***

2. ***Can you think of a situation in the near future that would give you an opportunity to work with these people?***

Summing up

The Creative Journey	Creative skills that help you in your journey	Blocks you may encounter	Values that might motivate you	Statements to build your confidence
Discover Purpose	*See the big picture*	*Apathy*	*Service*	*I make a difference!*
Assess Risks	*Take initiative*	*Status quo*	*Well-being*	*I am stimulated by uncertainty and challenge!*
Know Yourself	*Be open to new ways of doing things*	*Fear of failure*	*Peace*	*I am confident and creative!*
Analyze Priorities	*Look for input from others*	*Unable to define the real problem*	*Communication*	*I welcome diverse viewpoints!*
Develop Options	*Generate many options*	*Judging ideas*	*Creativity*	*I search for options with my mind and heart!*
Make Decisions	*Make decisions based on your values*	*Compromising too soon*	*Responsibility*	*I decide based on my values!*
Implement Plans	*Take action and be persistent*	*Not involving others*	*Quality*	*I persevere through thick and thin!*
Celebrate Results	*Share the credit and reward yourself and others*	*Not recognizing success*	*Truth*	*I am thankful for our success!*

TIP

These skills, values, and statements are useful throughout the Creative Journey. Even though we have suggested using them at a particular step, try out different ones whenever you think they may help you on your way.

"If there is a way to do it better... Find it!"

■ Thomas Alva Edison

TIP

To read more about the blocks and values for the Creative Journey, read Chapters 3 & 5 of *Flash of Brilliance: Inspiring Creativity Where You Work.*

"An idea that is not dangerous is unworthy of being called an idea at all."

■ DON MARQUIS

A challenge is a call to greatness. It is an opportunity to stretch yourself, test your limits, explore the unknown.

Challenges are provocative, stimulating ... risky. They summon our courage and focus our energy. They make our blood pulse, our senses quicken, our hearts race.

Daedalus longed for his freedom. King Minos imprisoned him in the labyrinth of the Minotaur. The island was surrounded by the sea.

Daedalus' challenge was provocative; how to outwit the king? Daedalus' challenge was stimulating; the promise of freedom. Daedalus' challenge was risky; if he failed, he and his son would die.

What exciting challenges do you face that provoke your mind, stimulate your emotions and are just a little bit risky?

Choosing Your Creative Journey

The purpose of this workbook is to help you find your personal source of creativity and motivate you to use it. And the best way to develop your personal creative potential is to try applying it to the real world.

This section marks the beginning of your Creative Journey. This is your chance to try out your creative ideas. At each step along the way you will learn the secrets to creative success. You will learn what you need to do, what blocks you can expect to come up against, and how to overcome them.

You'll find inspiration in reading about how others used their creative skills to make their mark upon the world. Questions will ask you to think not only about **what** you want to do, but **why** you want to do it. Exercises will help you figure out how to make your dreams come true.

And it's not all work; you'll have some fun along the way....

How to Complete Your Creative Journey

Four chapters of this workbook provide you with a step-by-step guide to **"Your Creative Journey"** (see pages 21, 47, 69, and 93).

They will show you how to:

- Discover the purpose of your creative efforts.
- Identify the scope of the challenge you face.
- Emotionally prepare yourself for the challenges you will face along the way.
- Be sure that you focus on the right situation.
- Involve others effectively to generate creative ideas.
- Find a breakthrough solution.
- Put your solution to work in the real world.
- Celebrate your success.

"Actions speak louder than words."

■ Anonymous

Apply What You Learn to Your Life

Each section will include a series of interactive exercises that will help you to plan and implement your journey.

These exercises may be questions to answer, forms to fill out, or checklists to check. They are designed to help you think through what you want to accomplish and why it's important.

Get your pencils ready and let's start your great adventure by choosing the creative challenge that you want to **do** something about.

What challenge — problem or opportunity — would you like to do something about?

Challenges you may want to consider are ones where

1. *You will deal with new situations.*
2. *You really care about being successful.*
3. *You will try out ideas that you haven't used before.*
4. *You can make a change.*

Examples of an appropriate situation might be:

- *Starting a new business.*
- *Adopting a child.*
- *Solving a perennial problem at work.*

Describe your challenge situation in words or pictures.

Write one sentence that says exactly what the problem is you want to solve.

I Make A Difference!

STEP 1

Discover Purpose

The first step of your creative journey is to discover your purpose. ***What do you want to do? Why do you want to do it?***

Your purpose or goal helps you figure out what you want to accomplish. It should be clear enough to provide you with a direction to follow, while still allowing for a sense of adventure in your journey. After all, half the fun of taking a trip are the surprises that happen along the way.

It may not be easy to get started, however. You may encounter an atmosphere of apathy. No one else may seem to care about what is going on. You may even be apathetic yourself, or feel burned out by the time you tried to change things in the past and weren't 100% successful.

At this point it helps to think about your commitment to **service.** Think about how your project has the potential to really contribute to your welfare and happiness. To realize how you can really make a difference in other people's lives, focus on how you can be of service.

KEY QUESTION: How can I best serve others and myself?

The Pathway Must Stay Flexible

"I go out into the future and figure out what it ought to be like , then turn around and see what the pathway is....

As a production organization, we're trying to design and develop commercially interesting, exciting, and successful entertainment and educational products using interactive technology. So that is the core business purpose; that's what we do.

But there is a bigger business purpose which is, to the extent that we can, to evolve the state of the art and to expand the accessibility of interactive experiences.

The pathway from here to there must stay flexible.

There is also an expression of another paradigm that's much more global, much more planetary, and much more collective than the specific thing we're doing, the specific project.

I'm at my best, my experience is at its height, and I am the most creative when I'm in both places at the same time. The reality of managing the day-to-day operations and the paradigm. This other state is much more intuitive and more collectively oriented. It is when I'm really looking at the global or evolutionary impact of everything. I try to play a little part in things broadening and expanding themselves in the whole process of Man growing up to be what Man is growing up to be."

■ Steve Arnold, Vice President, Lucasfilm, Ltd.

"When the history of our galaxy is written ... what will be worth recording is what kind of civilization we Earthlings created and whether or not we ventured out to other parts of the galaxy. It's human nature to stretch, to go, to see, to understand. Exploration is not a choice really, it's an imperative."

■ Astronaut Michael Collins, U.S.A.

"... We hold these truths to be self-evident, that all men are created equal, that they are endowed by their Creator with certain unalienable rights, that among these are life, liberty, and the pursuit of happiness ..."

In 1776, a group of men got together and came up with a clear purpose. The Declaration of Independence told the world in a few words exactly what they wanted to accomplish.

"... to institute new government, laying down its foundation on such principles, and organizing its powers in such form, as to them shall seem most likely to effect their safety and happiness...."

A statement of purpose is powerful. It sets the standard for how you and others think, act, and feel about what you do every day. It defines what is unique about what you want to accomplish. It helps you create a vision of how the world will be a little different once you have succeeded in your creative journey.

To get going, draw a symbol of the contribution you want to make in your Creative Journey.

"If a man knows not what harbor he seeks, any wind is the right wind."

■ SENECA

When the 56 congressional representatives signed the Declaration of Independence they told the world that they were ready to live by, and die for, their values. They believed that "all men are created equal" and were willing to risk imprisonment and war to make their dream come true.

Two hundred years later, we see that this was an idea whose time had come. But in 1776 it was new and unique and threatened the establishment. Taking responsibility for actualizing their dream required leadership, commitment, and sacrifice.

As you start on your Creative Journey, think about what is really motivating you to take on this challenge. You are taking on the responsibility for changing things and that may not always be easy.

To prepare for your role as leader, ask yourself:

What makes this challenge so exciting?

Once you've thought about the contribution you want to make and why you want to make it, it's time to define your purpose as clearly and concisely as possible. Write a goal statement that tells the world exactly how you plan to contribute to its welfare.

KEY QUESTION: What goal best serves others and myself?

T I P

By verbalizing your vision, you are giving others a chance to understand what you want to accomplish and the opportunity to join you in your adventure.

I am stimulated by uncertainty and challenge!

STEP 2

Assess Risks

The second step of your Creative Journey is to accept the uncertainty of change.

What is scary about this situation? What could go wrong?

The worst demons are the ones that you can't understand; the customer who suddenly cancels the order, the meetings you're not told about, the monsters under the bed....

When you are facing a new challenge, be ready to take some risks. Verbalize and accept the uncertainty in a new situation, and you take the first step to getting it under control.

Once you have made a commitment to taking on a creative challenge, two things are likely to get in your way — feeling too comfortable with the status quo or feeling too uncomfortable to risk doing anything about it. There is a natural resistance to change. It is easier and safer to stick with what has worked in the past than to risk trying something new.

If you feel a sense of inertia, it helps to take a hard look at your and others' future **well-being.** Even if things seem too OK, they may not be so great tomorrow. The biggest risk we can take in a fast changing world, is trying to hide our head in the sand. Try to perceive uncertainty as something positive and stimulating. Dare to be challenged by change, not afraid of it.

KEY QUESTION: How is our well-being at risk?

You're Not Licked Until You Quit

"I was the one who had to say 'No.' I was the one who had to say, 'Trust me.' I was the one who had to say, 'Once we get through this, then we are all going to win.'

I knew I was taking a risk. I knew the risk and I put myself out there... the worst thing I could do was cave in.

For the first six months I went home every night feeling sorry for myself. I had asked for more than I could swallow... At a very personal level, I felt inexperienced... I had feelings of just wanting to go away and hide somewhere ... of just going away and wrapping myself up in my mother's womb....

But over time I developed a certain sense of positiveness and perseverance. You're not licked until you quit. Positive expectations, positive visualization, positive outlooks have a lot to do with our results....

I had an excellent team to work with ... there was a sense of bonding beyond friendship or camaraderie. There was a sense of caring and sense of concern for everybody, for coming out of this hole as a whole organization. I even say a genuine sense of love between the parties, even though that was never expressed verbally...."

■ Dick Eppel, General Manager

"The thought that life and humankind might be unique in the endless universe ... compelled me to evaluate everything differently. Nature has been limitlessly kind to us, having helped humankind appear, stand up, and grow stronger. We have grown strong and powerful, yet how have we answered this goodness?"

■ Cosmonaut Yuri Glazkov, former Soviet Union

Imagine the uncertainty that Col. John Hunt faced as he and his men started up the steep slopes of Mount Everest. They had no maps to follow. They couldn't predict the weather. They didn't even know how far they would have to go. In fact, all they could count on to pull them through was their common purpose, their problem-solving ability, and the wisdom of their experience.

Hunt managed the risk and uncertainty of his adventure by gathering around him a team of experienced mountain climbers. Experienced climbers know that the way to get to the top is to pay close attention to what is going on around you, to be constantly watching your environment for signs of change.

As you start out on your Creative Journey, take a close look at your environment. What can your customers, boss, experts, co-workers or loved ones tell you? Gather as much information as possible about what is happening today and what everyone thinks will happen tomorrow.

Who should you talk to to educate you about your challenge?

- ☐ *The boss*
- ☐ *The mayor*
- ☐ *The cleaning lady*
- ☐ *The workers*
- ☐ *The boys in the backroom*
- ☐ *Your partners*
- ☐ *The captain of your ship*
- ☐ *Your secretaries*
- ☐ *Your spouse*
- ☐ *The product manager*
- ☐ *The designer*
- ☐ *The mad scientist*
- ☐ *The sales force*
- ☐ *The kids*
- ☐ *The customer*
- ☐ *The mailroom*
- ☐ *The team*
- ☐ *The expert*
- ☐ *The lawyer*
- ☐ *The bartender*

May 29, 1953 was the culminating moment for Col. Hunt's team. On that day a New Zealand beekeeper, Edmund Hillary, and a Sherpa guide, Tenzing Norkay, stood on the top of the world for the first time. Even though Hunt, himself, didn't make it to the top, his expedition succeeded where many had failed before.

There are many more outcomes to a successful climb than just making it to the top.

Hunt was concerned about the well-being of his team. He wanted to ensure that they all returned alive. He wanted to gather information about the mountain for maps. And he wanted to get at least one member of the team to the top of the mountain; not all of them.

When you start on a Creative Journey, it is important to consider how you will measure your success. Writing these criteria down will help you to define the scope of your journey. Remember, your journey's success is defined not only by what you accomplish, but also by what you learn along the way.

Write your criteria for a successful outcome of your journey.

Once you've considered what is going on in your environment and by what you will measure your success, you need to consider the well-being of yourself and the others that will join you on your journey.

How will what you are going to do impact the health, happiness, and prosperity of those around you?

What is the worst thing that could happen as a result of taking your Creative Journey?

What is the best thing that could happen as a result of taking your Creative Journey?

The answers to these questions will help you define the uncertainty you face. And understanding your fears is the first step to overcoming them. Ask yourself:

KEY QUESTION: How is our well-being at risk?

TIP

If you want to continue to work on your Creative Journey right away, go directly to "The Focus," page 59.

"The intelligent man's always open to new ideas. In fact, he looks for them."

■ Proverbs 18:15

We are all unique individuals. Each one of us has different habits, ways of expressing ourselves, talents, knowledge, values, and interests. And, while we all have the capacity to be creative, we like to approach change in different ways.

You may like to build on your past experience or maybe you prefer a vision to guide you. Maybe you're a fan of the scientific method or perhaps you like to throw caution to wind and explore the unknown.

Recognizing the different ways we like to express our creativity is the key to working together successfully.

We all have our own unique approach to meeting a creative challenge. We all have our own mixture of Innovation Styles.

Innovation Styles help us understand how we like to create. Each style represents a fundamentally different approach for managing the creative process.

Some people feel comfortable moving forward one step at a time; they like to build on what they already know is true and proven. They provide a team with the stability and thoroughness it needs to do a quality job. They emphasize the **Modifying** style.

Others like to focus on the end result. They have a vision of what they want to create. They are comfortable imagining an ideal result and then letting their goals be their guide. They can provide a team with direction, inspiration, and momentum. They emphasize the **Visioning** style.

Others like to experiment. Once they agree on a common process or way of thinking, they can troubleshoot anything. They contribute to the team by testing out new combinations of ideas and getting input from all concerned to ensure that everyone "buys into" the solution. They emphasize the **Experimenting** style.

And then there are those who just like to explore. These people thrive on the unknown and unpredictable. They like to use analogies and metaphors to come up with new ideas. They tend to add a sense of adventure to any project and open up the potential for dramatic breakthroughs. They emphasize the **Exploring** style.

How Does an Understanding of Innovation Styles Help You?

Learn something new every day. Discover your personal blend of the four Innovation Styles. Each style gives you a different way to meet new challenges creatively. By learning to use all four styles, you'll be more open, flexible, and self-confident when you take on a creative challenge.

Spice up your ideas. By recognizing and accepting creative differences, you can learn to take advantage of them. Seek a broader range of viewpoints and ideas when looking for new solutions. As you invite a wider variety of ideas and input into your life, your work will become more stimulating and interesting.

Build harmonious innovation teams. Each person you work with has a different blend of Innovation Styles. Once you understand how these styles influence their behavior, you'll understand them better. You'll be easier to work with and so will they.

Sell your ideas. Building creative relationships or having brilliant new ideas is only the starting point for the creative process. Action is the key to implementing them and making a real difference. An understanding of Innovation Styles can help you sell your ideas to others. Learn to speak their "language" and you'll be more effective in getting them to "buy in" to your creative ideas.

Help your organization become more successful. Organizations have a blend of Innovation Styles, too. Understanding your company's Innovation Styles pattern helps you manage its reaction to change and to your new ideas.

"Creative intelligence in its various forms and activities is what makes Man."

■ James Harvey Robinson

"Let's build on what we already have and make improvements where necessary."

People who take a Modifying approach to creativity are most comfortable working with facts and making decisions. They like to solve problems. They seek solutions by applying methods that have worked in the past. These people tend to be precise, effective, and reliable.

"I'm a pro. When someone asks me to do a job, they know they can count on it getting done on time and on budget ... Granted, I am conservative in my approach to managing my career. I try not to take on new responsibilities unless I am sure that, based on my past experience, I will be successful. This means climbing the ladder one rung at a time; it may not be the 'fast track', but it is getting to where I want to go all the same...."

■ Joe Shoe, Production Manager

Famous Modifying Examples

Gutenberg and His Printing Press

Before 1440, books were printed by hand using inked woodblock letters. Gutenburg modified this process by developing movable metal ones and fitting them into an adapted wine press. The result was the availability of books in quantity for the first time in history.

The Bill of Rights

Some people opposed the adoption of the U.S. Constitution because of its lack of guarantees of such rights as freedom of worship, speech, assembly, and the press. Supporters of the Constitution promised that if ratified, it would be amended in these respects. Accordingly, the original Constitution was modified in 1791 in order to strengthen its effectiveness as the law of the land.

Who do you know who emphasizes a Modifying style? When have you used this style?

"Let's develop a clear sense of purpose and goals to focus and drive the creative energy."

People who favor the Visioning style trust their instincts and like to make decisions. They seek solutions that focus on maximizing potential rather than focusing on what has gone on in the past. Driven by their long term goals and their organization's mission, they solve problems by relying on their vision of the future to guide them. This style is characterized by people who are persistent, hard-working and visionary.

"I know exactly what job I want in 5 years — Brand Manager. I can't wait to be in a position where I can really have a big impact on the success of the company... right now, being on the road five days a week, carrying a bag of samples may not seem to be the most glamorous of jobs, but that's OK, it is good experience. I'm learning what works with my customers, what they really need from us. No matter what, I'm making my numbers this year; then next year I'll have a shot at the Assistant Product Manager job in Marketing... it is all part of my master plan...."

■ John Merlin, Salesperson

Famous Visioning Examples

John F. Kennedy and the Man on the Moon

When John F. Kennedy set a goal for the United States to put a man on the moon in ten years, he gave us all something to work for. Millions of people aligned their personal visions with the dream of the nation and the result was not only Neil Armstrong's famous step for mankind, but the inventions of thousands of new products from Tang to Mylar.

The Magna Carta

In 1213 a group of English barons banded together with a common vision — to limit the absolute power of the king and to promise justice to all freemen in the kingdom. It took a few years of war to convince King James to agree, but in 1215, the Magna Carta was signed and our personal freedom has been protected by trial by jury ever since.

Who do you know who emphasizes a Visioning style? When have you used this style?

"Let's test one combination of things at a time, and assess the results. And let's get people involved to ensure a plan of action we can implement successfully."

The Experimenting style emphasizes fact-finding and information gathering. They seek solutions by applying pre-established processes and experimental trial and error. As problem solvers, they like to gather as many facts and opinions as possible before they make their decision. They are curious, practical, and good team players.

"I'm thrilled to be part of the management trainee program. I'm not really sure what I want to specialize in (my background is in research), but I've always been interested in marketing and general management as well... this program offers me a chance to work with a lot of different departments, before I have to decide exactly which one I want to be permanently assigned to... there is so much opportunity out there, I'm just lucky to get a first-hand taste of each one...."

■ Cris Columbine, Management Trainee

The United Nations

In June 1945, a war-weary world decided that there must be a better way to manage international disputes. Fifty delegates representing countries from around the world assembled in San Francisco and founded the United Nations. As a result, problems of global concern are discussed and opinions are shared before decisions are made.

Famous Experimenting Examples

Benjamin Franklin and His Kite

One summer's eve in 1752, Ben Franklin decided to prove that lightning was a manifestation of electricity. So he got out his kite, tied a key to one end of it and conducted his famous experiment. He proved his point by trial and error.

Who do you know who emphasizes an Experimenting style? When have you used this style?

"Let's explore in new directions and see where we end up."

People who take an exploring approach to being creative like using their insights to guide them. They like to gather lots of information in hopes that it will help them to approach problems from new angles. They tend to question assumptions and often will try to implement their ideas despite resistance from others. They are adventurous, challenging, and always on the go.

"You want to know the secret to my success? — cold calling... I know, everyone hates making cold calls. After all, who wants to get the door slammed in their face. But I have always found them a challenge; I'd treat them like they were some kind of great adventure. You never know when one of them will pay off, and when they do they tend to pay off big!... I guess I'm just lucky, but it seems that I am always able to find the right opportunity at the right time. Well, maybe I make my luck...."

■ Sue Piedmont, Salesperson

Famous Exploring Examples

Elias Howe and the Sewing Machine

Elias Howe spent years trying to invent a machine that would sew. Fueled by his vision of his future success, he sacrificed everything he owned, trying out new ideas. Finally, he gave up and went to sleep. He dreamt of his creditors dressed as savages coming to avenge his failure. They were attacking him with spears. But in his dream the spears had holes in their points. He awoke and his problem was solved.

George de Mestral and Velcro

During an Alpine hike in 1948 Swiss mountaineer, George de Mestral, was frustrated by the small prickly thistle balls that were seedpods for cocklebar bushes that clung to his pants and socks. While picking them off, however, he realized that if their clinging properties could be reproduced artificially, they would make great fasteners. Using the burrs as his simile, he succeeded in inventing Velcro ten years later.

Who do you know who emphasizes an Exploring style? When have you used this style?

Working Together

Even though you may have one primary Innovation Style, you have the seeds for all four styles as part of your makeup.

Each Innovation Style is like a language. While you probably feel comfortable speaking one or two languages well, you can benefit from learning to use all four.

Your own emphasis and blend of these four Innovation Styles is simply a way of describing how you feel most comfortable and capable in bringing about innovation and managing change in your life.

From the descriptions of all four styles, which is your favorite? Which is your least favored?

Questions the Modifying style loves to ask —

How can we build on what we already have?

Can we adapt this idea?

What would the experts say?

What's a short-term solution?

Questions the Visioning style loves to ask —

In a perfect world, what would this be?

Let's imagine that ...

How does this all fit together?

What is your long-term goal?

Questions the Experimenting style loves to ask —

How can we test it out?

What if we combined...?

Who's on board?

What's the process?

Questions the Exploring style loves to ask —

Why not?

Have you thought about starting from scratch?

What is this like?

What have we assumed here?

TIP

To get an accurate reading on your mixture of styles, the well-validated, Innovation Styles® self assessment is available. Contact www.creativeadvantage.com **for further information.**

Each Style Has its Pros and Cons

The Modifying style helps the creative process by finding practical ways to get things done quickly, but it can get in the way of progress by focusing on short-term realities and ignoring long-range opportunities.

The Visioning style provides "the big picture" and sets direction well; unfortunately, it can be so focused on the long-term goal, that other opportunities may be ignored.

The Experimenting style encourages communication and collaboration, but it also can get lost in the details and bogged down in following the procedures step-by-step.

The Exploring style loves to challenge assumptions and come up with "way out" ideas, but can lose interest when it comes to the details of planning.

"The road to the heart is the ear."

■ VOLTAIRE

How to Apply Innovation Styles

You can alter the wording of the basic questions according to the nature of the challenge.

Generate New Ideas

Increase the chance of finding break-through innovations by generating a broader set of creative options.

If you want to generate a broad range of ideas, start your brainstorming with the favorite questions of each Innovation Style.

- *Modifying: How can we adapt what we already have?*
- *Visioning: Can we imagine the ideal solution?*
- *Experimenting: What combinations can we come up with?*
- *Exploring: What is a metaphor for what we want to do?*

	Modifying	**Exploring**	**Visioning**
Basic "Compass" Questions	***What ideas could adapt or modify what we've done?***	***What ideas could start with totally new assumptions?***	***What ideas could give us an ideal future?***
Strategic Planning	*How can we build on our core strengths and capabilities?*	*How can we rewrite the rules of competition?*	*How can we be ideally positioned within the industry?*
Getting Ideas from Customers	*What could add to what you already have in place?*	*What could revolutionize the way things are done?*	*What could meet your long-term goals and strategy?*
Promoting Organizational Change	*What could improve on the best of what we've done?*	*What could shake up or unfreeze things, to see what emerges?*	*What could give us a world class organization (or process)?*

By understanding the four Innovation Styles, you'll be able to predict which approaches will work best for a particular group and tailor both the wording and the sequence for introducing each style to the group, thus helping assure everyone's full participation and the generation of a more comprehensive as well as creative set of solutions.

"You see things and say, 'Why?' I dream things that never were and say, 'Why not?'"

■ George Bernard Shaw

Experimenting

What ideas could combine different elements?

How can we synergize different technologies, partnerships, etc.?

What could be tested under trial circumstances?

What could give us the best synergy among our different units?

Become More Convincing

Improve how you sell your ideas based on a better understanding of how others — like your boss, your board, or your spouse — react to new ideas.

To sell your creative idea better, think about the Innovation Styles of the people who will have to "buy it."

If your idea is radical, people who favor the Exploring style will probably jump on your band wagon right away.

Visioning people will want to see exactly how your idea will help them achieve their goals before they show their support.

Experimenting people will examine how your idea gives them new choices and options in their work or take a consensus of everyone concerned before they commit.

And Modifying people will ask you about a million questions and make you prove your idea will work, but once committed, you can count on the all the way.

- *Who are the key people you need to support your Creative Journey and what is their style?*

Build Teams

Gain the participation of more diverse people in innovation projects.

In order to build more effective work groups, it is important to consider team members' Innovation Styles. Each person and each style will have a unique contribution to make.

- *What are the Innovation Styles of the people you want to involve in your Creative Journey?*

"I believe anyone can conquer fear by doing the things he fears to do."

■ Eleanor Roosevelt

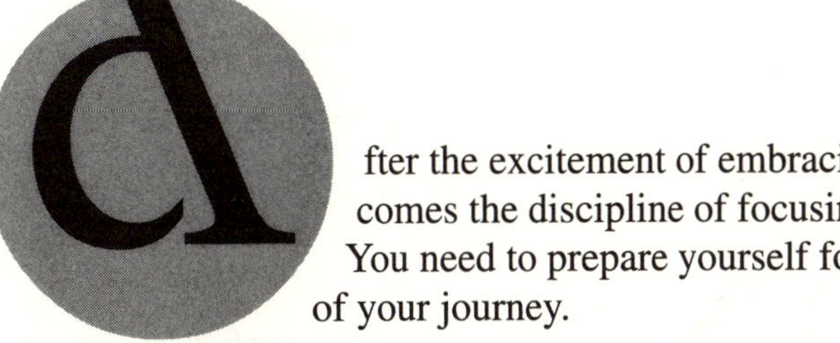

fter the excitement of embracing a challenge comes the discipline of focusing yourself. You need to prepare yourself for the demands of your journey.

To focus, tap into your character and find the courage you'll need to face the challenges ahead. Build on your past experiences and you will find the strength you need to go forward.

Have you identified the real problem or opportunity? Are you sure you're dealing with the cause of your situation and not just its symptoms?

Daedalus tapped into his character and found his way out of the Labyrinth despite the threat of the Minotaur.

Daedalus focused his situation and learned that it wasn't enough to escape from the Labyrinth. To really be free, he had to escape the island of Crete.

Do you have the courage to master your challenge?

I am confident and creative!

STEP 3

Know Yourself

The third step of your Creative Journey is to recognize what qualities you possess that will give you the strength to meet your challenge.

Why are you not afraid? What can you count on to pull you through the tough times?

As you progress in your Creative Journey, you are going to reach a crisis point where you just don't know if you're going to succeed. No one wants to fail or look dumb. You may feel overwhelmed by the enormity of the task or feel like it's all your responsibility and no one is going to support you.

At this point you need to stop, look inward, and re-establish your **peace of mind** and self-confidence about your project. Remind yourself that you've been in tight places before and managed to beat the odds. And if you have done it before you can do it again. This sense of self-confidence enables you to be more flexible and open-minded. Now you are really ready to apply your creativity to finding the solution to your challenge.

KEY QUESTION: What is the source of my peace of mind and self-confidence?

Let Us Wear Our Clothes Lightly

"As Martin Luther King said, 'We know finite disappointment, but we know infinite hope.' We have the sense that what we do makes a difference. It may not be in our lifetime, but there is hope and there are possibilities. I think that without hope, it doesn't happen.

" We wanted to create a low-income housing alternative to the welfare system. A group of us got together and said, 'Here is what we want to do in place of what is obviously not working.' We went to the governor's office and all of the bureaucrats sat there and said, 'You can't do that because of this and this and this and this ... and we said ... forget all the reasons why you can't do things and let's just do it....'

There is a value commitment that lets us wear our clothes lightly. When push comes to shove, there are other things that are more important to me ... like doing something that's going to make a difference, like being challenged, like seeing things happen, like people. They are more important than the salary, the physical things... it's a set of values that makes you freer in a lot of different situations and keeps you from getting hung up by the things that are going on."

■ Mary Nelson, President, Bethel New Life Corporation

"My mental boundaries expanded when I viewed the Earth against a black and uninviting vacuum, yet my country's rich traditions had conditioned me to look beyond man-made boundaries and prejudices. One does not have to undertake a space flight to come by this feeling."

■ Cosmonaut Rakesh Sharma, India

"I have a dream...it is a dream deeply rooted in the American Dream... I have a dream that one day in the red hills of Georgia, sons of former slaves and the sons of former slave owners will be able to sit down together at the table of brotherhood."

■ MARTIN LUTHER KING, JR.

The civil rights movement is one of America's most shining examples of how a group of people can decide to act upon their values and change things for the better. When Martin Luther King, Jr. spoke these words to the thousands of people who had come to Washington to demonstrate their support of civil rights, it was the culmination of a long and bitter struggle.

Anyone who was involved in the movement will remember its danger and challenge. Lynchings, beatings, and imprisonment were part of the everyday reality of the brave individuals who challenged the traditions of segregation. These people were afraid, but they didn't let their fear stop them. Their values gave them courage.

In your Creative Journey, your values will give you the courage you need to meet your challenge.

Which of my values will empower me through the tough times ahead?

Martin Luther King, Jr. was a preacher. He applied his oratory skills to converting a non-religious audience to his "dream" of an integrated America.

James Baldwin was a writer. He applied his talent to tell a compelling story to help the world understand the realities of living in a segregated society.

Marion Anderson was a singer. Her art allowed her to break the color barrier and sing at the Metropolitan Opera and show the world that segregation robbed everyone of their dignity.

None of these influential people were politicians, lawyers or sociologists, yet they managed to make a significant contribution to a sociopolitical movement that changed American life. They applied their creative talents and experience to meeting the challenge of civil rights in their own unique way.

As you look at what your challenge will require, it helps to take stock of what unique talents and experience you bring to it.

TIP

Once you are confident in your ability to meet the demands of this challenge, you will find that you can afford to be much more flexible and open to new ideas.

1. Review the list of successful outcomes you made in Step Two (pages 42-45). Select the two outcomes that are most important to your success.

2. List three specific examples of tasks you will have to do to achieve your successful outcome.

3. Recall and note a previous experience or talent you can apply that will help you accomplish this task.

Outcomes	***Tasks***	***Talents/Experience***
1. ______	______	______
	______	______
	______	______
2. ______	______	______
	______	______
	______	______

You will have to call upon the moral strength you get from your values and your unique blend of talent and experience to get you through the tough times ahead. As a leader of a compelling cause, others will look to you to provide a sense of harmony and direction. And you won't be able to give that to others unless you are in control of your own peace of mind and sense of self-worth.

To prepare for your Creative Journey, ask yourself ...

KEY QUESTION: What is the source of my peace of mind and self-confidence?

I welcome diverse viewpoints!

STEP 4

Analyze Priorities

The fourth step of your Creative Journey is to engage the situation.

What is the real problem or opportunity? What do others have to say about it?

The first thing you have to do when you begin searching for your solution is get a clear definition of exactly what problem you want to solve, or which opportunity you want to develop. Be sure you are dealing with the cause and not the symptoms of your problem or promises of your opportunity.

At this point you may find that everyone has a different opinion of what the problem or opportunity is, what is causing it, and what needs to be done about it. Patiently listening to everyone's opinion can be very frustrating.

The key to making it through these trying times is to remember the value of **communication.** Although the last thing you may want to do at this point is sit through a lot of long, drawn-out meetings, it is important to make sure that everyone gets to contribute their two cents. Welcome diverse viewpoints and gather all of the information you need to be sure that you engage the right situation.

KEY QUESTION: Based on what everyone has communicated, what is the real problem?

Program Managers Don't Design Cars, Teams Do.

"The people working on the program loved to dump all the critical information on the program manager. They would feed everything up and then think the program manager would solve all the problems that they should handle. I didn't like that. I thought the information should be totally shared throughout the whole program and by the entire program team, because the team is responsible for putting the program together.

I struggled with the fact that in Japan executives don't have offices; they work amongst the people, they work with the people. So I decided to move the project to a basement location. Nobody had an office. Everybody had equal areas. I felt, as the program manager, I was just as important as my chassis manager, as my designers... I wanted to make sure there wasn't any class distinction. I wanted a large open environment with the vehicles in the center; so we would be able to focus on the cars....

We had a central communication area that was unique...we took a pillar in the center of the work area and put a series of information boards together so all the competitive information, all the body information, all the chassis information, and all the customer information was in the central board area. Everyone had to feed their information into this central area ... the team owned the information, not just the program manager. That's important because the team is going to make the car for you. Program managers don't design cars, teams do."

■ Sue Gatchell, Director of Quality Network
General Motors Corporation

"The first day or so we all pointed to our countries. The third or fourth day we were pointing to our continents. By the fifth day we were aware of only one Earth."

■ Astronaut Sultan Bin Salman al-Saud,
The Kingdom of Saudi Arabia

By the time he was 28, Mozart was considered a has-been by the court of Franz Joseph. Although he had already composed "The Marriage of Figaro" and "Eine Kleine Nachtmusik," he was considered temperamental and a troublemaker. His royal commissions had stopped and his aristocratic audience no longer wanted to hear his music.

Down on his luck and penniless, he turned to a friend who came up with the bright idea for Mozart to write an opera for the theater of the working class. No one had ever thought of entertaining the masses with a comic opera before. Skeptical, but desperate, Mozart embraced the idea and wrote "The Magic Flute," the opera for which he is most loved and famous.

When you are trying to engage the situation, it helps to get input from as many people as possible. Go beyond your immediate work team or peer group and search out others who might have a fresh insight on your problem or opportunity.

Who should I talk to about my problem/opportunity?

What do they think the real problem/opportunity is?

As you are defining your problem/opportunity, make sure that you are tackling a situation that you can handle. You don't want to choose a situation that is way beyond your power to do anything about like:

- Change the tastes, prejudices, and politics of the Court of Franz Joseph.

or you may have defined your problem too narrowly, like:

- How to make enough money from the concert to pay off my debts.

when your real problem is:

- How to adapt the art form of opera to entertain and please a new audience.

To make sure you are tackling the right size problem/opportunity situation, try out this exercise:

1. ***Write what you think the goal is on the center line of the Triangle diagram.***
2. ***Ask yourself: "Why do I want to resolve or develop this situation?" and write your answer above your first statement. This will give you a broader definition of your situation.***
3. ***Ask yourself, "What is getting in my way?" and write your answer below your first statement. This will narrow the focus of your situation.***
4. ***Pick which of the three statements best describes the situation you feel ready to handle.***

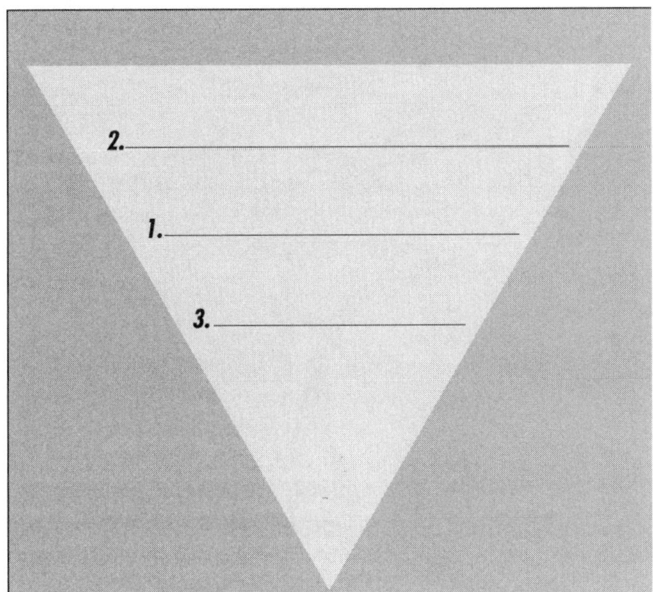

Now combine what you have learned from everyone else with your insight into how much of the challenge you want to tackle, and define your problem/opportunity.

KEY QUESTION: Based on what everyone has communicated, what is the real problem?

TIP

If you want to continue working on your Creative Journey, go directly to "The Solution" on page 83 of this book.

"The way to get good ideas is to get lots of ideas and throw the bad ones away."

■ Linus Pauling

There are thousands of ways to generate ideas.

Robert Frost used to take long nature walks for inspiration. Albert Einstein used to go to bed and dream about his theories. Archimedes made his greatest discovery while stepping into his bath. Madame Curie locked herself in her laboratory and experimented for four years.

Each of us has our own special recipe for cooking up new ideas. Some people like to work with others, some of us are loners. Some like to do a lot of analysis, others like to daydream.

It doesn't matter what you do to get your creative juices flowing, as long as you do it. But to help you along your way, this chapter shows you how to do a number of techniques you may not have tried before.

Brainstorming

Before you even start to generate ideas, it helps to lay some ground rules. By setting up some guidelines, you will find that your brainstorming sessions are much more productive. They will help to prevent conflicts before they happen, and make everyone feel more comfortable and open to contributing their great ideas.

Guidelines for Effective Brainstorming

- ***See the big picture.***
  Stretch yourself to see the big picture.
- ***Take initiative.***
  Say your ideas as soon as you think of them.
- ***Be open to new ways of doing things.***
  Take a risk. Half-baked ideas are OK.
- ***Look for input from others.***
  Encourage everyone in the group to contribute.
- ***Generate many options.***
  Use both sides of your brain.
- ***Make decisions based on your values.***
  Don't judge your or anyone else's ideas.
- ***Take action and be persistent.***
  Keep pushing; generate as many ideas as possible.
- ***Share the credit and reward yourself and others.***
  Build on each other's ideas.

TIP

These guidelines for effective brainstorming are built around the eight creative skills. Following them will help you to practice your skills.

For more information and examples on idea generation techniques, refer to Chapters 9 and 10 of *Flash of Brilliance: Inspiring Creativity Where You Work.*

Your Innovation Style is based on how you like to use information to stimulate your creativity. Each Innovation Style prefers a different methodology for generating and evaluating ideas. The preference is illustrated by the basic question posed when faced with a creative challenge.

- The Visioning Style likes to ask:
  What can we realistically visualize as the ideal solution over the long term?
- The Modifying Style likes to ask:
  What can we adapt to improve upon what has worked before?
- The Experimenting Style likes to ask:
  What ideas can we combine and test?
- The Exploring Style likes to ask:
  What metaphors can we use to challenge our assumptions?

There are many different idea-generation techniques based on the methodologies of the four different styles. This section of the workbook introduces four techniques, each representing one of the styles.

Visualize

For the Visioning Style, the workbook shows you how to do **Realistic Day-dreaming**, a technique that emphasizes using your imagination to write an ideal future solution.

Adapt

For the Modifying Style, the workbook shows you how to do a **Force Field Analysis**, a technique emphasizing adaptations to improve a situation.

Combine

For the Experimenting Style, the workbook shows you how to use a technique called **Random Idea-Generation** which will help you come up with novel combinations of ideas based on key variables.

Symbolize

For the Exploring Style, the workbook will give you a chance to use pictures to develop metaphors and get new insights and ideas in a technique called **Photo Symbols.** This technique is called **Guided Imagery**.

Put Them All Together

Finally, you will find a technique that will help you stimulate more ideas by jumping from one Innovation Style to another. This is called the **Compass** technique.

TIP

It is helpful to use all four Innovation Styles' methodologies in order to ensure that you will have a wide range of new ideas. If you don't have the time to try out all four, then be sure to do at least two techniques using *opposite* styles — e.g. Modifying and Exploring techniques and Visioning and Experimenting techniques.

Realistic Daydreaming

Realistic Daydreaming is a technique that helps you figure out where you want to end up. It gives you a snapshot of the future by having you verbalize what you really want to happen.

1. ***Describe the subject about which you want to generate ideas.***
2. ***Take a minute to close your eyes and relax.***
3. ***Read the following scenario.***

   Imagine some time in the future. You are reading an article reporting on the results of the task you are working on now.

   The article heralds the significant achievements of your efforts. It reports on the positive social and economic impact of your accomplishments.

   As you read the article, you realize that everything that you have ever wanted to happen about this project has come true. Even the impossible dreams have become a reality. Describe what you have read.

   The last part of the article tells what had to happen to reach this wonderful conclusion. It lists the key milestones in the project's progress. Describe some.

4. ***Describe your accomplishments described in the text of the article.***
5. ***Now see if you can generate some more specific ideas around your accomplishment.***

The accomplishments described in the article ...

Accomplishment:

Specific Ideas:

Accomplishment:

Specific Ideas:

Accomplishment:

Specific Ideas:

Accomplishment:

Specific Ideas:

Force Field Analysis

Force Field Analysis helps to identify forces that contribute to or hinder a solution to a problem. Force Field Analysis helps you identify strong points in a situation as well as the problem areas. These strong points can be the foundation of the most effective solutions, which might have otherwise been overlooked.

1. ***Pick a situation you would like to see changed:***

   For example: your product line, work conditions, or relationship with your boss.

2. ***Write a brief statement of the problem you have to solve.***

3. ***Describe what the situation would be like if everything fell apart — absolute catastrophe.***

4. ***Now describe what the situation would be like if it were ideal.***

5. ***Presume the center line represents your current situation. "Catastrophe" and "Ideal" are playing a tug of war. Fill in what forces are tugging right now at your situation to help make it more ideal and what forces are trying right now to make it more catastrophic.***

Problem

____

Catastrophe ______________________________ **Ideal** ______________________________

Forces

◄ ______________________________ ______________________________ ►

◄ ______________________________ ______________________________ ►

◄ ______________________________ ______________________________ ►

◄ ______________________________ ______________________________ ►

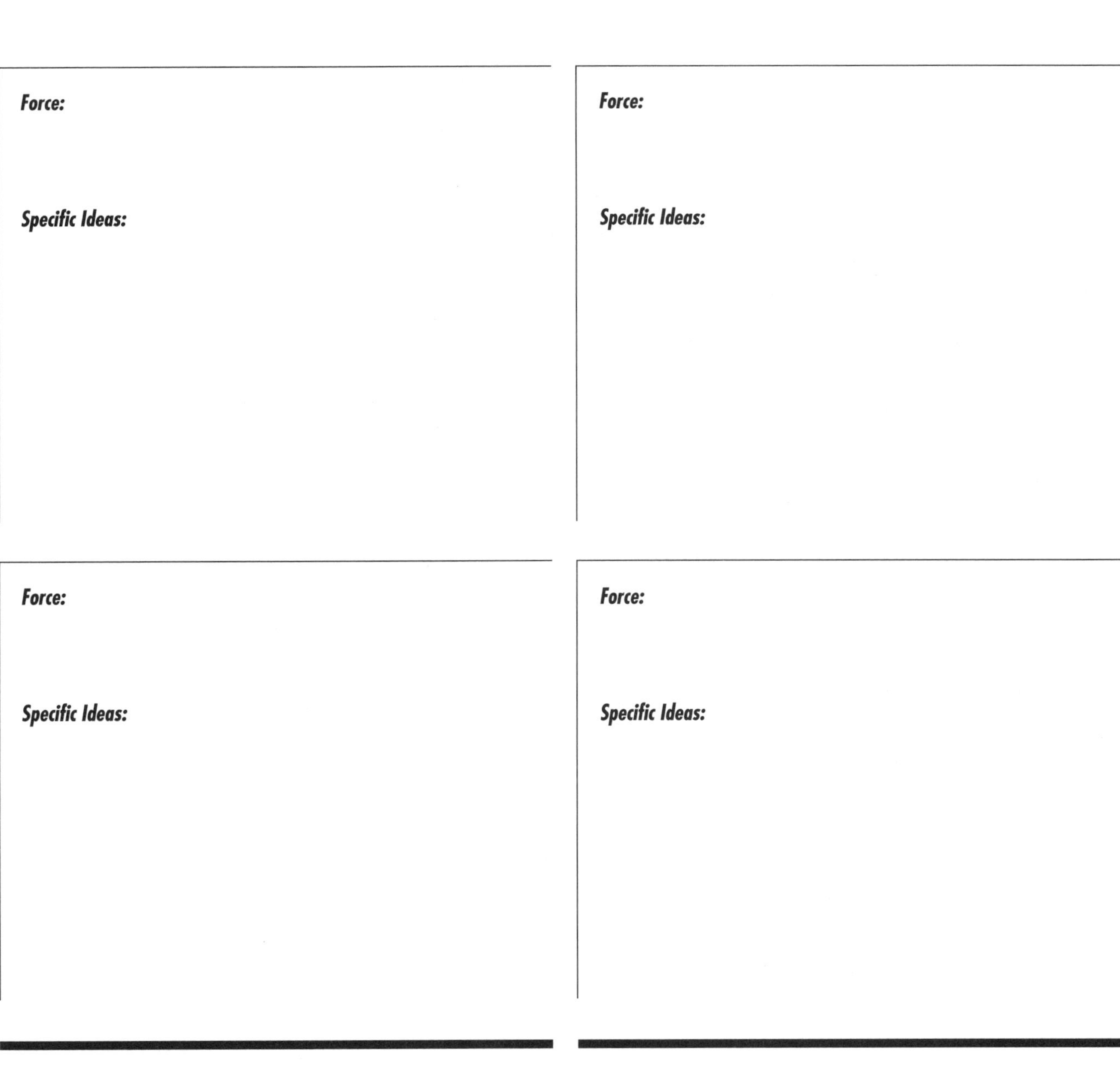
Force:
Specific Ideas:
Force:
Specific Ideas:
Force:
Specific Ideas:
Force:
Specific Ideas:

Random Idea-Generation (Morphological Analysis) is a fun way to combine partial ideas into whole ones. The results can be silly or practical. Either way, the combinations can spark new ideas to solve your problem if you let them.

1. ***Identify the key variables in your problem. List them across the top of a matrix.***

   For example:
   If you were trying to invent a new food product, your variables could include:

KINDS	FORMS	PROPERTIES	PACKAGING

2. ***Brainstorm all of the possibilities under each variable. List them underneath the key variable.***

   For example:
   The possibilities for each key food variable would include:

KINDS	FORMS	PROPERTIES	PACKAGING
1. Meat	*Drink*	*Medicinal*	*Bottle*
2. Fruit	*Flake*	*Odor*	*Box*
3. Grain	*Soup*	*Taste*	*Sack*

3. ***Randomly combine any item from the first column with any item from each of the other columns.***

   For example —
   A fruit soup with medicinal properties, packaged in small sacks ...

KINDS	FORMS	PROPERTIES	PACKAGING
1. Meat	*Drink*	*Medicinal*	*Bottle*
2. Fruit	*Flake*	*Odor*	*Box*
3. Grain	*Soup*	*Taste*	*Sack*

4. ***Now try to generate some more specific ideas based on your combinations of properties.***

VARIABLES				
1.				
2.				
3.				
4.				

Combination:

Specific Ideas:

Combination:

Specific Ideas:

Combination:

Specific Ideas:

Combination:

Specific Ideas:

Photo-Symbol

Photo-Symbol can help you find new insights into the nature of a problem and new solutions for resolving it. This exercise uses symbolic metaphors to help you gain a new perspective on your creative challenge.

Metaphors presesent the possibility that two conditions or things might be similar even if they appear dissimilar on the surface.

For example

How is a relationship between two people like a pencil?

Well ...

How is a solution to my task In some way like this photo?

It would be nice to be able to erase mistakes.

Specific Ideas:

What is inside a relationship can be more important than how it appears to the outside world.

It would be nice to be able to erase mistakes.

It can be used to make a statement in the world, etc.

Using metaphors, you can often find new insights into the nature of a problem and new solutions for resolving it. Metaphors help to "make the familiar strange, and the strange familiar."

1. ***Using a camera and a roll of ten exposures, take a few pictures representing two of the following ten values:***

Service	*Well-being*
Communication	*Peace*
Creativity	*Truth*
Quality	*Responsibility*
Excellence	*Love*

2. ***Use the photos as symbolic metaphors for developing some new solutions to your task by asking:***

   How is a solution to my task in some way like this photo?

3. ***Try to generate some more specific ideas based on your metaphorical idea.***

(Paste Photo Here)

How is a solution to my task in some way like this photo?

Specific Ideas:

How is a solution to my task in some way like this photo?

Specific Ideas:

Compass Technique

In this exercise you will use four different creative approaches in order to generate as many ideas as possible. Each one of the ideas will help you to consider your challenge in a new way. They will help you to try using:

- The Modifying Style by asking:
  What can we adapt to improve upon what has worked before?
- The Visioning Style by asking:
  What can we realistically visualize as the ideal solution over the long term?
- The Experimenting Style by asking:
  What ideas can we combine and test?
- The Exploring Style by asking:
  What metaphors can we use to challenge our assumptions?

1. Use the questions that represent each Innovation Style to spark your thinking and brainstorming ideas. Generate at least four ideas using each question.

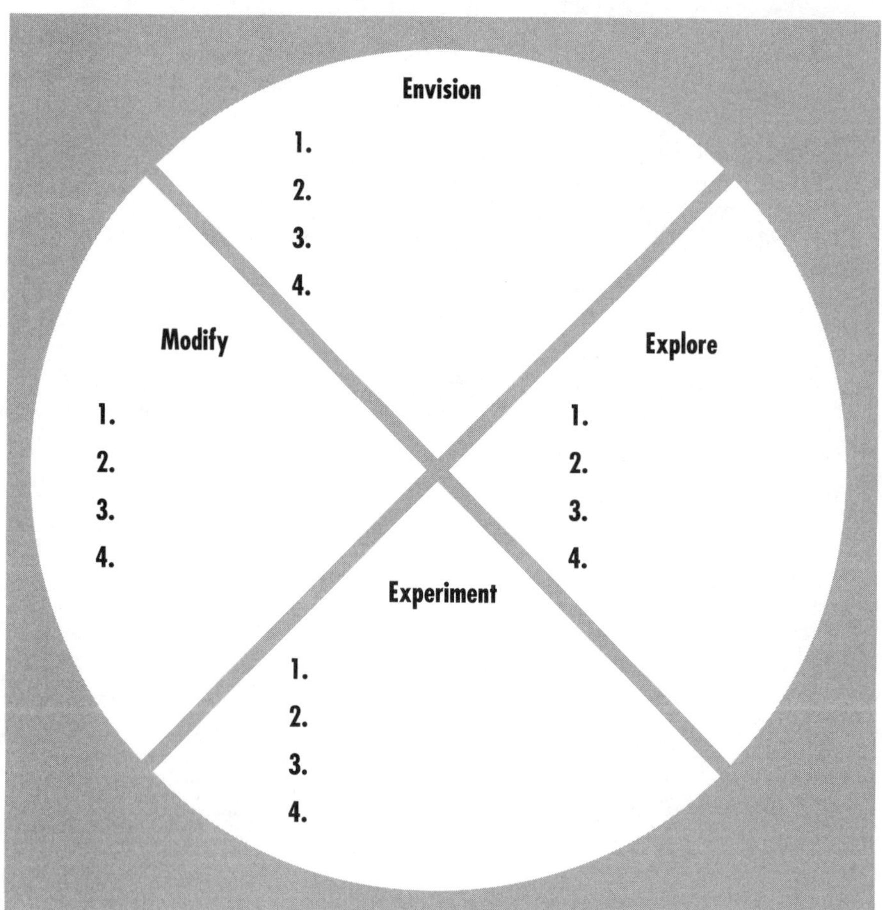

T I P

By knowing The Innovation Style preferences in a group, you can introduce different techniques and questions to satisfy everyone.

"When I feel that the top of my head has been taken off, then I know it's poetry."

■ Emily Dickinson

Building good solutions is exciting. It is a chance to explore new possibilities, brainstorm ideas and find a breakthrough.

Finding the best solutions can take a lot of effort, too. It requires patience, flexibility, and a single-minded devotion to finding the answer — the right idea. It invites us to exceed our expectations. It challenges us to do our best. It frustrates us when they don't show up on time.

Daedalus had to get off the island. King Minos ruled the sea. The sky was his only hope. Daedalus' solution required patience — the answer wasn't obvious. It required flexibility — Man couldn't fly. It was a breakthrough — to become a bird and fly to freedom.

Considering your challenge, are you ready to search for the best solution?

I search for options with my intuition, mind, and heart!

STEP 5

Develop Options

The fifth step of your Creative Journey is to develop as many new ideas as you possibly can.

What could we do? What would be fun to do?

This is the fun part of your Creative Journey. It is your chance to be wild and crazy. Brainstorm with others. Laugh a lot. Have some fun.

When you are developing options you need to be as inventive as you possibly can. The more ideas and alternatives you can develop the better. So be careful not to stop too soon or to judge the quality of the ideas before they have a chance to prove themselves.

If you find that your ability to generate more solutions is getting bogged down, it helps to remind yourself that you are trying to come up with a **creative** solution; one that is truly unique and has not been tried before. Exercise not only your mind, but your intuition and heart too. You may be surprised with how many ideas you can come up with.

KEY QUESTION: Using both heart and mind, what are some creative options?

The 12-second Pit Stop

"We videotaped our first changeover and it was very interesting. It is like putting eyes in the back of your head. The things you do when you are on the line is routine ... 'this is the way I have always done it, and I haven't looked at new or faster ways of doing a changeover in years.'

Our approach was, This is the way we do our changeovers.' There is nothing wrong with the way we do them. We do them like every other PVC plant in the U.S. But is this the right way? Should we be doing them this way? Can we do them better? Can we make this look like an Indy pit stop?

One of our dye men said he was watching a NASCAR race over the weekend. They showed a film clip of a pit stop back in 1974. They did it in 35 seconds. It was pretty phenomenal.... they thought they were doing great. And then they showed a pit change this year and it was 12 seconds! Now we're not talking a whole lot of time, but every second is crucial and the same analogy holds true for us.

So, we just talked about some things we could do to do our changeovers better. 'What about this?' 'What if we used that?' 'What if we put the right tools in the right spot?...' we just started asking the questions. Just by planting the seeds, people have enough initiative on their own to start to make things better.

A year ago it took us 45 minutes for a changeover, now we can do it in five or six minutes."

■ Joe Worklan, Plant Manager, PW Pipe

"'Not a day without a discovery' was our motto during the mission. If we were unable to make a discovery in our experiments, then we would discover what was for lunch."

■ Cosmonaut Vladimir Kovalyonok, former Soviet Union

"I was thrown out of college for cheating on the metaphysics exam; I looked into the soul of the boy next to me."
■ Woody Allen

"Gray hair is God's graffiti."
■ Bill Cosby

"The trouble with the rat race is that even if you win you're still a rat."
■ Lily Tomlin

Woody Allen, Bill Cosby, and Lily Tomlin have delighted millions of people with their unique sense of humor. By showing us our quirks and foibles in a lighthearted way, comedians invite us to reconsider our opinions about ourselves and the world we live in.

Humor is a great way to spark new ideas. It gets you thinking differently about your problems. By juxtaposing ideas that don't logically belong together, a joke can open your mind up to a whole new world of possibilities.

As you prepare to develop options for your solution, you want to gather information that will help you to spark new ideas. This information could include reports, articles, pictures, cartoons, famous quotes or even a book of jokes.

What information do I need to stimulate new ideas and perspectives for achieving my goal?

Including different kinds of people in your idea-generation sessions is also a good idea. For example, you might want to include customers, tech reps, experts, artists, workers, or kids in order to get some fresh ideas.

There are lots of good techniques available to help you generate ideas. As you plan your brainstorming session, be sure to include techniques that encourage you to think both intuitively and analytically. Using both sides of your brain helps you come up with ideas that appeal to both your heart and mind.

A good way to ensure that you consider all the aspects of your situation is to include at least one technique from each of the four Innovation Leadership Styles. Remember to Adapt, Combine, Imagine, and Symbolize.

You'll probably generate hundreds of ideas from your various brainstorming activities. Choose a few that are truly unique. Make sure they not only make sense but feel right as well.

Who should I involve in my brainstorming sessions?

KEY QUESTION: Using both heart and mind, what are some creative options?

I decide based on my values!

STEP 6

Make Decisions

The sixth step of your Creative Journey is to find the breakthrough solution that will solve your problem or take advantage of your opportunity

What feels right? What do you just "know" will work?

After the fun of brainstorming, selecting your solution can be hard. By now you probably have come up with some very innovative ideas that you think are just great, but they may be just a little ahead of their time.

Don't be tempted to compromise too soon because you are concerned that your boss will think you are crazy to propose such a wild idea.

If you feel like you are about to settle on a less innovative solution in the interest of making it more "acceptable", take the time to tap into your sense of **responsibility.** This is your project and you are accountable for its outcome. If you really believe your "way out" idea will work, then you can probably convince others as well.

Make your decision based on your deepest personal values. In the long run you will be more committed to seeing it succeed, and happier as well.

KEY QUESTION: What solution is most <u>responsible</u> to myself, my goal, and our well-being?

A Whale of an Idea

"When we were working on the Altima seat for Pontiac ... everyone was very satisfied with the progress ... but we were having a tremendous problem with what is called a 'closeout.'

... a closeout is where a piece of plastic comes together with a piece of material. The problem was especially difficult in the side of the driver's seat because it has moving side-bolsters. The movement is very complex because you're not just moving around a cylinder, but actually moving dynamically in several directions. The movement caused a big gap that possibly could trap the hands of a child.

We worked on the problem for over six months and we couldn't come up with an answer. We tried everything that we could possibly think of... we were really at our wits' end to come up with an idea.

One day I was out in the Catalina channels sailing and thinking about this problem. I was lying back on the deck with a beer in my hand and a California grey whale came up beside the boat. It came out of the water and took a big breath. That's a fairly awesome experience.

And that did it. I glanced over at the belly of the whale with its fluted structure expanding and contracting, and I said to myself 'That's it!' That's the answer. If a whale can breathe and have its fluted structure expand and contract, then certainly we can have the closeout detail move in the same fashion as the belly of the whale."

■ John Gooden, Vice President of Marketing and Design, Design West, Inc.

"A Chinese tale tells of some men, sent to harm a young girl who, upon seeing her beauty, became her protectors rather than her violators. That's how I felt seeing the Earth for the first time. I could not help but love and cherish her."

■ Astronaut Taylor Wang, China/USA

Christopher Columbus tried to convince a lot of people that the world was round before he finally found someone to back his "crazy" idea.

Queen Isabella was intrigued by the Italian adventurer and his heretic idea that the world was not flat. Unfortunately, her husband and banker were not. So she decided to sell her jewels to finance Colombus' venture to find a new route to the Orient.

Isabella made a daring decision when she chose to back Columbus. Her country's future prosperity depended on her finding safe trade routes to the Orient. By knowing what she wanted to accomplish, she was able to make a "breakthrough" decision.

Taking some time out at this point to re-evaluate exactly what you want to achieve can help you evaluate your many ideas and pick the best ones for your solution.

1. ***Refer back to the successful outcomes you listed in Step 2 (pages 42-45), and how you defined your problem/opportunity situation in Step 4 (pages 64-67).***
2. ***Next develop a list of decision criteria that will help you evaluate your ideas in light of what you want to accomplish. Be sure to include your values in your list of criteria.***
3. ***Evaluate how well your creative ideas from Step 5 satisfy your criteria using +, 0, -.***

Ideas	***Criteria***			
	A.	**B.**	**C.**	**D.**
1.				
2.				
3.				
4.				
5.				
6.				

The tough part about making a creative decision is that there are no sure answers. Often it requires a leap of faith. Even though Columbus was convincing, Isabella wasn't 100% sure that the world was round. But, by being able to accept the uncertainty, her decision allowed for a breakthrough to happen.

One way to help minimize the uncertainty is to choose an option that has the potential for both a short and long term success. The riches that Colombus brought back from his first trip to the New World helped Isabella to finance more extensive explorations.

When you are developing a creative solution, consider both the long and short term impact of your decision. Evaluate each idea for its short term feasibility as well as its potential to produce a truly novel and productive solution over the long haul.

By now you probably have a few favorite solutions. Before you make your final decision, however, look at each one and ask yourself if you are ready to be held accountable for it and its impact on those around you.

TIP

If you want to continue working on your Creative Journey, go directly to "The Completion" on page 109 of this book.

List your favorite solutions.	*How could it work in the short term?*	*Over the long term?*

KEY QUESTION: What solutions are most responsible to the goal and our well-being?

"A good leader who talks little when his work is done, his aim fulfilled, they will say 'We did it ourselves.'"

■ Lao-Tzu

As you become more skilled at expressing your personal creativity, you become more self-confident. You look for opportunities to exercise your creative muscle. Challenges are more inviting, uncertainty is more exciting and your solutions become more creative.

Putting your creativity to work means tapping into others' creativity as well. Many people are afraid to express their creativity. They think someone will tell them their new idea is stupid or they're afraid to rock the boat. They're stuck in a rut.

Armed with your creative confidence, you have a lot of personal power. Extra energy. So why not help others? Invite them to join you on your Creative Journey. Show them how to make things happen. Share your success with them. And you'll probably find that they start to become more confident and skilled as well.

Playing in Tune Together

When was the last time you attended a live musical event… to listen to an orchestra concert, a rock band, a jazz group, or whatever? When musicians play the same piece of music, at the same rhythm, each player with their own role… that's alignment. In business, *alignment* means agreeing on goals, roles, decision power, and work processes.

But before musicians begin to play their first song, what must they do? Tune their instruments. If they don't, their music will be very unpleasant, even if they start and finish the same piece together. Professional musicians wouldn't dream of performing without being in tune. Yet, in the work world, we play together all the time without being tuned up. In business, *attunement* means resonating with the individual purpose and relationship values of each person.

To get the highest creativity and productivity from a group, you must promote both alignment and attunement. Alignment gives single-*mindedness* of purpose. Attunement gives single-*heartedness* of purpose.

Here's an overview of the key questions to discuss and resolve for each issue:

ISSUE	***KEY ISSUES TO EXPLORE AND AGREE ON***
ALIGNMENT	
Purpose and Vision	*What is our charter (purpose, vision, scope)?* *What is our mission and authority?*
Roles	*What do we expect of each person, especially in terms of responsibilities?* *What does each of us bring to the team? (Watch out for isolating a person as the sole resource for a specific strength.)* *Do we have the right mix of talent for what we need to do?*
Empowerment	*What authority to make decisions and act does our team, and individual members, have?* *When do we get involved in the course of major decisions — how early?*
Processes	*What are our ground rules for communicating, resolving conflict, generating ideas, making decisions, and giving each other feedback?* *How do we share knowledge across sectors?* *How do we make sure the best ideas rise to the top?*
ATTUNEMENT	
Personal Purpose	*How can we support each other in living our personal purposes at work?* *How can we operate our group by the combined set of our individual purposes?*
Personal Values	*What can people do to create greater authenticity and caring as the basis of their relationships with each other?* *How can we apply our own best experiences in teams to build better relationships with each other?*

If your group wants to start off on the right foot, or has communications problems, start with personal purpose and interpersonal relationships; only after that will alignment group purpose, roles, empowerment, and processes be possible.

If your group has previously formed close relationships with each other, or are extremely task-focused and won't stand for this "soft stuff," start aligning on task-oriented issues; leave personal purpose and interpersonal relations to the end.

It is often wise to have a skilled, outside facilitator to act as a catalyst, guide, and arbitrator in resolving especially sticky issues.

Teamwork and innovation is best nurtured by the harmony of head and heart. We must align and attune ourselves with each other if we are to have peak-performing groups (including large groups called *organizations*). "Feel with your minds, think with your hearts" is an appropriate motto for successful, innovative work.

TIP

For more specific ideas about how to align and attune a team on all the key issues, see chapter 7 of *Flash of Brilliance: Inspiring Creativity Where You Work.*

Start the Team's Creative Process

As you progress in your Creative Journey, you'll find that you are involving more and more people in your quest. While you searched for your solution, you involved other people to help you generate ideas. In the next leg of your journey, you will be soliciting the help of still more people as you try to implement your ideas.

In order to make your plan happen, you need the support and help of many people. You'll probably go to your boss or banker and ask them for money. You'll approach your colleagues and co-workers asking them to donate their time and energy. You'll ask your support staff or friends or family to do you favors. In short, you'll gather a team around you to help you get the job done.

Building a team is a challenge, especially the kind of team that sticks with you through thick and thin in order to make your novel idea work. You have to be inspiring. You have to be confident. Even if you aren't the boss, you have to become a leader.

Moving from "I" to "We"

As you progress in your Creative Journey, you have seen that certain statements help you feel more confident and powerful in each step of the process. 0When you are trying to involve others in your creative efforts, it is important to share that self-confidence with others and encourage them to feel as strongly as you do.

You'll want to change the "I" in your statements to "WE."

How a Creative Team Feels

We make a difference!

We are stimulated by uncertainty and challenge!

We are confident and creative!

We welcome diverse viewpoints!

We search for options with our hearts and minds!

We decide based on our values!

We persevere through thick and thin!

We are thankful for our success!

"You have to do what you say you are going to do; you have to act the way you say you are going to act, and you have to demonstrate that every day in every way. People will test and challenge you. They will ask you questions that will test your moral fiber and will test your values system. They will test the truth of your vision. They will test your resolve. They will test all of that and you have to work through it every day."

■ Dick Eppel, General Manager

Recognizing a Creative Team

Your creative team is on a journey like you are. And just as you need to individually develop your creative skills to be more effective, the team needs to develop its skills as well.

Look to your creative skills to guide you through the challenge of building a creative team around you. These skills will help you set the stage for creative collaboration.

- As you help them to see the big picture, the team will begin to share a common vision.
- As you help them to become more aware of their future well-being and encourage them to take initiative, the team will become more interested in questioning the status quo.
- As you demonstrate an open attitude to new ideas, the team will feel comfortable in taking more risks.
- As you actively seek out others' opinions, the team will be more eager to collaborate.
- As you encourage them to try out new ways to generate ideas, your team will become more comfortable in using both their intuition and analysis to develop many options.
- As you rely on your values to make your decisions, your team will work harder to find a breakthrough.
- As you are persistent in implementing the solution, your team will stick by you when the going gets tough.
- As you reward and recognize everyone's contribution, your team will feel better about themselves and join you in your celebration.

Be a force in spreading your confidence to others, so each person in your work group recognizes their own creative potential and puts it to use.

The next few pages will help you use your creative skills to help you build a more creative team. Even if you are not the leader of the team, the following questions and exercises can help you make a big difference in how your team operates creatively.

STEP 1

To get going on your Creative Journey use your ability to see the big picture to figure out what you want to accomplish and why it is important. Once you sort all that out, you are ready to go out and make a difference.

Creative teams need to feel challenged as well. They have to share your dream. Your idea could bring new meaning and purpose to their lives. Show them how your goals and values relate to their own.

Once you do, you'll probably be surprised by how supportive they become. They'll play with your idea as if it was their own. They will start to try it out, tinker with it, and probably come up with some new ideas of their own. But don't let that scare you; the new ideas won't replace yours, just improve it.

EXERCISE FOR DEVELOPING AN ATTITUDE OF LEARNING AND PERSONAL CHALLENGE FOR YOUR TEAM.

1. ***Ask each member of your team to say in turn, one important way he/she wants to develop his/her professional or personal skills over the coming year.***
2. ***Record each person's developmental goal. Then look for ways to incorporate it into accomplishing the team's tasks.***

QUESTIONS TO ASK THE TEAM WHEN THEY ARE DISCOVERING THEIR PURPOSE.

- *What is your initial goal?*
- *Who do you want to serve, and how?*
- *What goal are you most passionate about?*
- *What would make any hardship worthwhile?*
- *What goal allows you to best exercise your talents?*
- *What are you afraid to wish for?*
- *How can you best express your life's purpose here?*

"One person with a belief is equal to a force of ninety-nine who only have interests.

■ Anonymous

STEP 2 As you face the risk and uncertainty of your challenge, you have to be stimulating. Let your concern for the well-being of others inspire you to take the initiative to do something. Face up to your challenge and discover how it can excite and motivate you.

It is important that your team feel they can take initiative as well. Creative teams have a certain energy about them; a liveliness that makes things happen. As a member of a creative team, be ready to be constantly surprised. As you start to unleash the creativity of those around you, wonderful things are going to start to happen. You need to encourage them when they do.

EXERCISE TO HELP THE TEAM EMBRACE A BROADER PERSPECTIVE ON THE IMPORTANCE OF THEIR CHALLENGE AND THE UNCERTAINTY THEY FACE.

1. ***Ask each person to select a different magazine that is relevant to the team's challenge.***
2. ***Each person should review the issues from the past year and select articles that are relevant to the team's task.***
3. ***Each person should summarize the articles in writing, then circulate them.***
4. ***Hold a team meeting where you all discuss the research and how it could influence their project.***

QUESTIONS TO ASK THE TEAM WHEN THEY ARE MEETING UNCERTAINTY.

- *What risks do you face?*
- *What's at stake? What makes it a difficult challenge?*
- *What do you fear in this situation?*
- *What could be the negative consequences of success?*
- *What past failures do you most want to avoid recreating?*
- *What are you afraid others will think of you if you fail? If you succeed?*
- *What prejudices might keep you from seeing the situation objectively?*

STEP 3

To prepare for your Creative Journey, you look for ways to maintain your peace of mind and self-confidence to carry you through the frustrating moments. This makes you flexible and open to new ways of doing things.

Share your attitude of flexibility and openness with your team. It will establish an atmosphere of trust. Set a standard for straightforward communication and encourage risk-taking. If people are afraid of failure or reprisals, they are not going to come forth with new ideas or risk their jobs to make your idea work. They need to feel that you are behind them every step of the way.

EXERCISE TO HELP THE TEAM IDENTIFY THEIR RANGE OF TALENTS AND BUILD THEIR SELF-CONFIDENCE ABOUT BECOMING ACTIVE, CONTRIBUTING TEAM MEMBERS.

1. ***For each member of the team, write their name on the top of a 3" x 5" card. Make up and distribute a set of cards to each.***
2. ***Ask each team member to identify a key talent, skill, or knowledge each person can contribute to the team in meeting its challenge.***
3. ***All at once, have the team give each other all of his/her cards.***
4. ***Ask each person to read all their cards out loud and comments as they wish.***

QUESTIONS TO ASK THE TEAM WHEN THEY ARE COMING TO KNOW THEMSELVES.

- *What values do we have to empower us through the tough times ahead?*
- *What talent and experiences do we bring to help us achieve our purpose?*
- *What is the source of our peace of mind and self-confidence?*
- *What gives **you** confidence in yourself?*
- *How can you handle the pressures you're going to face?*
- *What gives you the courage to succeed?*
- *Where does your faith in yourself and others come from?*
- *What skills do you have for drawing out the best in others?*
- *What personal values are most important for you to act upon?*
- *What is the opportunity here for personal and professional growth?*

TIP

If people feel shy, ask the group to reaffirm the positive contributions each person makes.

STEP 4 When you are trying to engage the situation, make a special effort to seek out everyone's opinion. By opening up the floor for discussion, you are able to identify the cause of the real problem or opportunity. If you don't, you'll end up wasting your time dealing with its symptoms.

A creative team needs to be able to openly discuss ideas. There needs to be a spirit of debate. You can't have rational discussions when there is a lot of emotional anguish and ownership of ideas. You need to set the stage for low emotional conflict. This means that everyone is entitled to their opinion. Everyone gets to say what's on their minds. And then ideas are generated and decisions are made based on the cause of the problem, not its symptoms.

EXERCISE TO HELP THE TEAM PLAN AHEAD FOR DIFFERENCES IN WORKING STYLE.

1. ***Have each team member complete an Innovation Styles Profile, available from the Global Creativity Corporation.***
2. ***Ask each team member to share their profile with their teammates.***
3. ***Discuss ways to make the mixture of your Innovation Styles preference work to the team's advantage.***

QUESTIONS TO ASK THE TEAM WHEN THEY ARE ENGAGING THEIR SITUATION.

- *How would other people, inside or outside the organization, restate our purpose in their own terms?*
- *How broadly or narrowly should we define the problem?*
- *Based on what everyone has communicated, what is the real problem?*
- *What are the priority issues to be resolved?*
- *What would other stakeholders say are their key concerns?*
- *What are the primary barriers to overcome?*
- *What is the hidden truth about this situation?*
- *Where does your intuition tell you to focus your attention?*

- *What truth is the hardest to accept?*
- *What new knowledge is needed to understand this situation?*
- *How can you keep from (a) oversimplifying the situation or (b) getting bogged down in its complexity?*

STEP 5 When you generate ideas, you need to be as inventive as possible. You call upon your feelings, intuition, and mind to generate as many options as you can. It helps to have a good time while you are trying to come up with new ideas. You want to laugh a little, joke around and try to come up with some really wild ideas.

Teams need to have fun, too. Good creative teams are spontaneous and lively. When they get together there is a relaxed atmosphere, everyone has a good time. Encourage this atmosphere. Have a meeting in a bar. Invite a clown. Let the good times roll.

EXERCISE TO HELP THE TEAM GET IN TOUCH WITH THEIR IDEAL SOLUTION BEFORE A BRAINSTORMING SESSION.

1. ***Review the Guidelines for Effective Brainstorming. See page 70.***
2. ***Do a "warm up" brainstorming exercise.***

   For example: Name a living thing (like a bird, animal, plant, fish, etc.) and generate as many ideas as possible for how it is symbolic of:

   - *The nature of the problem.*
   - *Possible idea solutions.*
   - *A logo for the team.*

QUESTIONS TO ASK THE TEAM WHEN THEY ARE DEVELOPING OPTIONS.

- *What is the most critical information for stimulating new ideas and perspectives for achieving our goal?*
- *Based on the different Innovation Styles approaches to idea-generation what can we come up with — Modifying? Visioning? Experimenting? Exploring?*
- *Using both our hearts and minds, what are some creative options?*
- *What creative ideas can you generate?*
- *What ideas give an ideal solution?*
- *What ideas start with totally new assumptions?*
- *What ideas build upon what you've done?*
- *What ideas combine different elements?*
- *What ideas want to emerge on their own?*
- *What are some unique, unusual, or absurd ideas?*
- *What are some ideas that are exciting, satisfying, surprising, or humorous?*

STEP 6

When you search for your breakthrough solution, you'll evaluate many options and choose the one that has the most promise. Sometimes, making a good decision means not deciding too soon or going ahead with what you've got and then seeing how it flies.

Creative teams need time to generate and develop their ideas. Sometimes the best thing you can do as a leader is just let everyone be. Give them time to muck around with their ideas. At other times, the deadline cannot wait. You'll need to push for the best available solution and wait to improve it later.

"I do not look,

I find."

■ Pablo Picasso

EXERCISE TO HELP THE TEAM GET IN TOUCH WITH THEIR VALUES BEFORE THEY EVALUATE THEIR IDEAS.

1. ***Ask each team member to make of list of five to ten "values" they find very important in their life, like honesty, family, security, adventure, love, etc.***
2. ***Have them select three values that are their highest priority. Then have them choose the one value out of these three that they would like to have the opportunity to exercise in their work.***
3. ***In turn, each person should talk about this value and explain to the group what it means to them.***

QUESTIONS TO ASK THE TEAM WHEN THEY ARE TRYING TO FIND THEIR BREAKTHROUGH.

- *What alternatives would work in the short term? What are its potential contributions over the long term?*
- *What are the criteria of my intuitive and analytical mind and my heart?*
- *What solutions are most responsible to the goal and our well-being?*
- *What options do you choose?*
- *What are your criteria for a wise choice?*
- *Intuitively, what is most likely to work?*
- *What are sustainable, long-term solutions? Some quick wins?*
- *What's the hidden gem, whose advantages are not obvious?*
- *What are the advantages of others' favorite ideas?*
- *What ideas are you willing to fight for?*
- *What solution "stands for" the values you most cherish?*
- *What solution are you most afraid of?*

STEP 7 When it comes time to implement your idea, be committed to its success. Don't let anything stand in your way. No matter what the obstacles, persevere in order to make your idea come true. Of course you may find yourself breaking a few rules, stepping on a few toes, and working a few late nights to make your idea work.

In order to help you in your quest, creative teams need to have the freedom to act. Expect to make mid-course corrections. Use your plan to keep your team focused, but don't hamper their progress. Keep them focused on the goal, but let **them** implement the plan.

"A good leader takes a little more than his share of the blame, a little less than his share of the credit."

■ Arnold Glasow

EXERCISE TO HELP THE TEAM SUSTAIN ITS MOMENTUM DURING THE IMPLEMENTATION PHASE BY GETTING AND GIVING SUPPORT.

1. ***Ask each person to note a few, specific types of support they most want to receive over the life of the project.***
2. ***Also note a few specific types of support they feel good about giving.***
3. ***Have each person share their ideas with the rest of the team.***
4. ***Ask for volunteers to provide the support that each member of the team needs.***

QUESTIONS TO ASK THE TEAM WHEN THEY ARE IMPLEMENTING THEIR PLAN.

- *What is the best plan for gaining support for and implementing our solution?*
- *What resources — financial, time, human, information, etc.— are needed to implement the plan?*
- *How can we implement our solution in a high quality way?*
- *What will you do to implement your solution?*
- *What is the hidden wisdom in the objections that people raise?*
- *What has to be "let go of" to succeed?*
- *What is the right timing for action?*
- *Where will you need to push hard — or be flexible — for successful implementation?*
- *What commitments are you, or others, likely to miss if you aren't impeccable keeping agreements?*
- *What shift is needed for people to embrace the solution?*

STEP 8 When you have finally reached your goal, take the time to recognize and celebrate your success. A job has been well done; progress has been made. Congratulations!

Before you break up and go on your merry way, take the time to share with each other what you have accomplished. As a team, you've shared a lot of laughs and tears, and you have probably learned a lot from each other, too.

As the leader of the pack, thank and reward everyone who helped you along the way. Take the time to single out each contributor. Figure out what kind of recognition would mean the most to them. And then invite them to share in your success.

EXERCISE TO HELP THE TEAM MAINTAIN ENTHUSIASM, MOTIVATION, AND RAPPORT WHILE MEETING THEIR CHALLENGE.

1. ***Periodically, have a group meeting where each team member states how the experience he/she is getting on the project is contributing to his/her professional/ personal goals.***
2. ***In the same meeting, ask each team member to talk about what has happened for which they are grateful.***

QUESTIONS TO ASK THE TEAM WHEN THEY ARE CELEBRATING THEIR RESULTS.

- *What impact have we had? In the short term? Toward our long term goal?*
- *In what ways could we celebrate our success in a meaningful way?*
- *How shall we celebrate the truth of what we accomplished?*
- *What are the results, and your satisfaction from them?*
- *What are the benefits to stakeholders?*
- *What rewards and satisfactions do you want?*
- *How can you share the credit with those who deserve it?*
- *How are you richer as a person from what you have learned?*
- *What would you have done differently?*
- *What important, new knowledge can be gained?*
- *How can you bring others "up to speed" on new knowledge, information, and insights?*
- *When will you know it's time to celebrate? Time to move on?*

At the end of your adventure together, take the time to look once again at the big picture. Talk about how you have changed and share what you want to do next. You've made some good friends on this journey, and you may want to include them on another one in the future. Lay the groundwork now, so you won't lose touch.

EXERCISE TO HELP THE TEAM BUILD A FEELING OF ONGOING SUPPORT, EVEN IF THEY ARE DISBANDING AT THE END OF THE PROJECT.

1. ***Ask each person to restate the value they wanted to use in their work which they identified at the beginning of the project.***
2. ***In turn, discuss how the group incorporated that value into the work they did together.***
3. ***Brainstorm specific ways that the groups or individual team members could continue to exercise the value in the future.***

QUESTIONS TO ASK THE TEAM WHEN THEY ARE REDISCOVERING THEIR PURPOSE.

- *How did our journey embody the value of excellence each step of the way?*
- *How did we embody the value of love and caring?*
- *Considering all we have learned, how can we best serve others and ourselves?*

"Treat people as if they were what they ought to be, and you help them become what they are capable of being."

■ Johann Wolfgang Von Goethe

TIP

For more information about building a creative team, read Chapters 6,7, & 8 of *Flash of Brilliance: Inspiring Creativity When You Work.*

"It's real simple."
STEP B73
L5
FIG.6
P6
STEP IIC
FG2

"A diamond is a piece of coal that stuck to the job."

■ Anonymous

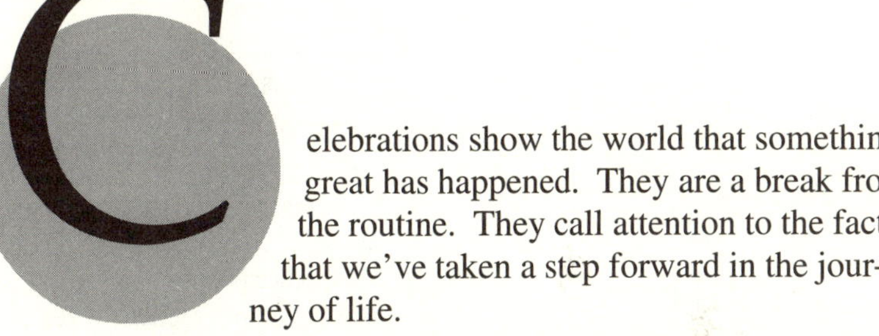

Celebrations show the world that something great has happened. They are a break from the routine. They call attention to the fact that we've taken a step forward in the journey of life.

Implementing a novel idea is a celebration in itself. It isn't always fun and easy, but it is enriching our lives. It is meeting our challenge and being victorious.

Daedalus gathered thousands of feathers. He fashioned great wings. He flew to his freedom.

To move on, we must leave things behind. A celebration marks our passage. It applauds what we have learned and accomplished in the past, and puts it to bed. It frees us to move forward.

As a result of your Creative Journey, you'll change.

What's next?

I persevere through thick and thin!

STEP 7

Implement Plans

The seventh step of your Creative Journey is to implement your solution.

How will this idea work in the real world? How can I get others to accept and support this idea?

Now that you have come up with a solution, it is time to test it out in the real world. The key to developing a plan to implement your solution is flexibility. Listen carefully to what other people have to say, and be willing to modify your wonderful idea in order to make it more practical or feasible.

For many people, making their idea work in the real world is the toughest part of the Creative Journey. You have to convince others that your idea will work. You need to build a support network. You need to get other people to contribute their time, energy, and money to help you implement your solution. And you may not get this support right away; it may take years of persistent persuasion and sweat to realize your dream.

It helps at this point to make a commitment to **quality**. Your creative idea is unique and deserves to be implemented in the best way possible. Since you are going to have to persevere through thick and thin, you might as well do it right.

KEY QUESTION: How can I implement this solution in a high quality way?

Breaking the Rules

"We had to come up with an implementation approach that broke the rules. I remember sitting in front of a council representing the UAW and plant management saying, 'Yes gentlemen, I understand that you are going to spend ten million dollars on building and implementing this training program, but I feel very strongly that you shouldn't require people to attend. Make the program available to them, but let them volunteer to take it. If they are forced to attend, it won't work.'

And they looked at me like I was absolutely crazy and said, 'You expect us to spend all this money and not require people to go through it?'

And I said, 'Yup, if the program works you will have word-of-mouth advertising in the plant and people will be eager to sign up for the program.' Actually, it turned out to be the perfect approach. Workers are very independent people. You don't tell them what to do.

When they ran the program in the plant, the number of grievances went up because the workers said their bosses weren't letting them go through the program as quickly as they wanted to. The first people who went through the program had a good time and they realized it was a valuable experience. They went back and told their friends and then their friends wanted to go, too.

The volunteer approach, which was different than what you normally do, broke a rule. But it was also the key to the program's success."

■ Janice Van Collie, Instructional Designer

"The first shoots came up in our garden. The pea plant comes out of the soil with a fat stem and tightly wrapped leaves. The wheat just shoots up like a ray of green light. I like running my palms over the shoots. They tickle."

■ Cosmonaut Valentin Lebedev, former Soviet Union

"Even sleeping beside those thin stems was better."

■ Cosmonaut Georgi Grechko, former Soviet Union

Imagine the resistance that a 16 year-old, illiterate peasant girl faced when she presented the Dauphin of France with her plan to drive the English out of France and make him king. Fortunately, she had her faith on her side.

The story of Joan of Arc is one episode after another of winning support for her bold plans. Led by her "voices," she led the French to a series of major victories over the invading English army and laid the groundwork for the unification of France.

Needless to say, in the beginning she didn't get much support. She wanted to liberate Orleans; the generals said it was impossible. She wanted to unite France; the Dukes said it had never been done before. She believed it was her divine calling; the Church said she was a heretic and burned her at the stake.

Although you'll probably have an easier time of it than Joan did, expect some resistance to implementing your novel idea. If your idea calls for sweeping changes, it may be threatening to the status quo. If your idea is unusual, it may be difficult for others to understand. If you are unusual, you might find it difficult to get people to even listen to you.

So to get your great idea off the ground, you'll need to plan how to do it, and how to get others to buy into its successful implementation.

How can I get others to support my solution? Who will it impact? Why should they support it?

Who will benefit?

To free France, Joan had to raise an army.

To implement your idea, you are going to need resources — time, money, equipment, people, information, etc. Finding those resources and convincing others to invest in your idea can be an exhausting process.

You'll probably feel that you will never have enough time or money to do the job perfectly. But most likely you'll find a way to make do with what you have and still see your idea succeed. It helps, however, to ask for enough resources up front so you don't find yourself halfway through your plan having to make unacceptable compromises because you have run out of resources.

Take the time to develop a detailed plan, schedule, and budget for your implementation. Make sure that your plan considers both tangible and intangible resources. Use the checklist below to make sure that you consider all the resources you might need to make your dream come true.

Money

- ☐ *Ready cash*
- ☐ *Investment capital*
- ☐ *Operating expenses*

Time

- ☐ *Your time*
- ☐ *Your boss's time*
- ☐ *Quality time*

People

- ☐ *Expert advice*
- ☐ *Technical support*
- ☐ *Administrative support*
- ☐ *Emotional support*
- ☐ *Political support*
- ☐ *Life support*

Information

- ☐ *Research reports*
- ☐ *Public information*

Materials

- ☐ *Raw materials*
- ☐ *Supplies*

Technology/Equipment

- ☐ *Computers*
- ☐ *Specialized equipment*
- ☐ *Telecommunications*

Other

- ☐ *Good working environment*
- ☐ *Transportation*
- ☐ *Take-out food*

Before you finalize your plan, take a long hard look at whether it accommodates your need for a high quality implementation. Although you are going to need to be flexible, don't let your dream die by making too many compromises along the way.

KEY QUESTION: How can I implement the solution in a high quality way?

I am thankful for our success!

S T E P

8

Celebrate Results

The eighth step of your Creative Journey is to take the time out to recognize and celebrate your success.

What have we accomplished? How are we better off because of our efforts?

You've made it. You have finally seen your dream come true. Have you stopped to recognize your and your collaborators' accomplishments? Lots of creative people don't take the time to acknowledge their success. They are always rushing on to meet the next challenge and eventually they get burned out.

Sharing and celebrating your success is an important part of your Creative Journey. Not only does it feel good, but it gives you a chance to recognize and learn from your experience.

Take the time to look at the **truth** of what you have achieved. What have you accomplished that is positive and good? Share this truth with others. Not only will it feel good, but it will inspire others and yourself to move on to greater challenges with a renewed sense of purpose.

KEY QUESTION: How can I celebrate the <u>truth</u> of what we've accomplished?

Nine months of growing

"About a year and one-half ago we started to look at total quality....

At the end of nine months, we concluded our efforts with a presentation by the people who had done the job. These people included some line people from the plant, some clerk folks from administration...in fact, there were only two executives on the team. The presentation was to the president of the corporation.

The presentation was done by a team of four people, and they were probably the lowest people in the organization. What was creative about it was that we didn't say ahead of time who was going to present the findings. In a hierarchical environment like Pillsbury, people assumed that the two vice-presidents on the committee were the ones who were going to do the presentation. But they didn't. The element of surprise in a situation like that is very useful; particularly when people make assumptions about other folks' abilities.

I wanted to prove the point that people working together for a period of nine months grow. They grow in knowledge and they grow in self-esteem."

■ Anthony Harris, Human Resources Manager, Pillsbury Company

"The peaks were the recognition that it is a harmonious, purposeful, creating universe. The valleys came in recognizing that humanity wasn't behaving in accordance with that knowledge."

■ Astronaut Edgar Mitchell, USA

Andrew Jackson, the seventh president of the United States, was the first man to win the presidency primarily through his appeal to the mass of the voters rather than through the support of the political establishment. He was a self-made man from the West, and his victory symbolized the triumph of political democracy.

And when he won, he decided to throw a party. Jackson's inaugural ball went on for three days. To the horror of society he invited everyone who had contributed to his successful campaign, and thousands showed up. A grand time was had by all, and the populist spirit behind American politics was born.

In your journey, you probably won't have an event as obvious as an election victory to mark your success. But you don't want to miss the opportunity to celebrate your accomplishments and reward the people who have contributed along the way. So, start to plan your celebration by taking the time to reflect on the impact you have had so far.

What impact have I had so far?

In each step of the journey, you have looked to others for ideas and support. Now is the time to recognize not only your success, but the contributions everyone else has made as well.

Rewards are only effective when they are appropriate. Whether you are trying to come up with a way to pat yourself or someone else on the back, you need to think about what kind of reward would be most satisfying. There are lots of different ways you can reward a job well done. Use this chart to figure out a new way to reward the key people on your innovative team.

1. ***Review the list of Satisfiers to get an idea of the broad range of ways you could reward someone.***
2. ***For each person you want to reward, choose a Satisfier category you feel they would find most valuable.***
3. ***Come up with a specific idea for a reward for each person.***

Satisfiers

- **Self-determination:** greater control, flexibility, independence
- **Advancement:** more influence, better use of talent, promotion
- **Training and Development:** opportunity for personal growth
- **Intrinsic:** more satisfaction, greater self-esteem
- **Social:** working with important, enjoyable, stimulating people
- **Financial:** more money, greater comfort
- **Impact:** recognizable achievement, sense of service
- **Environment:** better working conditions
- **Recognition:** greater respect, feeling special
- **Security:** more secure in job, better position

Person	*Satisfier*	*Specific idea for reward*

TIP

Come up with both a short and long-term milestone to symbolize your success. Your short-term celebration might give you the extra boost you need to persevere over the long haul.

Before you start to celebrate take a moment to sincerely think about what you have accomplished.

What have you learned from this experience?

How are you a different person?

How is the world a slightly better place thanks to what you have accomplished?

KEY QUESTION: How can we celebrate the truth of what we've accomplished?

Now you really have a reason to party!

I have new contributions to make!

S T E P

1

(Re)discover Purpose

The final step of your Creative Journey is to begin again.

What have I learned about myself? What do I want to do next?

Success breeds success. Once you have succeeded in meeting one challenge, you feel empowered by having proven to yourself that you are creative and capable of making a difference. You have grown. You have more insights, more skills, more gifts, and more confidence to put into your next adventure.

And what if it didn't turn out the way you wanted? Well, the past is gone and you have learned something valuable for the next time.

Even if you are eager to get going on your next adventure, take a moment to think about how you have changed. Re-examine your creative experience with a critical eye.

Have your values changed? What is most important to you now? What do you really want to be doing?

Look around you. Does your current job or environment support your new aspirations? Do you need to change things before you can really start your next Creative Journey?

Reconsider your commitment to service. Based on the value of excellence, how do your new ideas have the potential to really contribute to the welfare and happiness of others or yourself? How can you show them you really care?

KEY QUESTION: Considering all that I have learned, how can I best serve others and myself?

Love is Letting Go of Fears

"What came out of the experience of the journey to the moon was the enormous sense of responsibility that goes with the power of creativity. What happened for me was the awareness that it is an individual responsibility. It can not be put off to 'out there' or 'they' or 'somebody else.' We each have to accept our creative potential and our ability for intelligent activity, and we have to accept the responsibility that goes with it.

We have to accept the responsibility for our lives. This is something our belief systems of the past have not forced us to do. We have been able to say, 'No, that's "God's" problem.' If we recognize what we are in the creative process that has caused us to be where we are on this planet, then we have to accept the responsibility that goes with it.

The word responsibility means to accept one's choices and the consequences of one's choices, with that goes the notion of becoming proactive instead of reactive. In our earlier times, living systems were mostly reactive. They reacted to fear. We are trying to become proactive toward our lives and the future and that means letting go of the fear.

Love is letting go of fears. With that comes the sense of responsiveness that you use ... or the sense of responsibility that you use ... to take charge of your own life. Take charge of your fears and automatically that brings a deeper sense of love and responsibility for one's self, one's environment, and one's planet."

■ Edgar Mitchell, Astronaut, NASA

"From space I see myself as one more person among the millions and millions who lived, lives, and will live on Earth. Inevitably, this makes one think about our existence and the way in which we should live to enjoy, to share, our short lives as fully as possible."

■ Astronaut Rodolfo Neri-Vela, Mexico

"Two roads diverged in a yellow wood, and I — I took the one less traveled by, and that has made all the difference."

■ Robert Frost

You have been on a journey. You have assessed your creative potential, explored new ideas, examined your values, and imagined your future. Now it's time to **choose** your insights to make a difference.

What do you really get when you choose to live up to your creative potential?

Your life is more interesting. You get a chance to focus on what is important to you. You have the power to have an impact on other people's lives. You can make the world a little better place.

What else do you want?

So, take a chance. Try exercising those creative muscles. You'll be surprised by how much fun it is.

Have you ever watched the face of an Olympic skier just before a big run down the ski slopes? Or a diver just before going off the 10-meter board? You are likely to see their eyes closed and an intense look of concentration on their face. What are they doing?

They are mentally rehearsing the ideal result of their efforts — the fastest run, the perfect dive.

These athletes know that mind fitness is as important as physical fitness. Like them, you can prepare yourself for your creative adventures by mentally rehearsing your success.

Throughout this program you have been affirming how it feels to exercise your creativity. You have also learned how to do various visualization techniques which help you picture your success. To mentally rehearse your success as an effective creative person, you need to take three simple steps.

1. ***Relax your body and mind so they become ready to learn how it will feel to reach your ideal goal.***
2. ***Imagine your ideal outcome. Draw a picture in your mind's eye of exactly what you want to accomplish. Focus in on the details, so you can really feel your success. Let it come alive!***
3. ***Create a statement that communicates how you feel in one simple, short, concise sentence. This statement should tell you where you are going. Word it in the present tense to bring it alive. Make it rich in detail.***

Focus on one of the creative skills you want to develop. Imagine how it will feel to be a master of this skill. Remind yourself how wonderful you will feel when you have accomplished your goal.

Draw what you want to accomplish.

Create a statement that communicates how you feel.

Our Final Thoughts

There is much for us to do together to bring about the quality of work life that we know is possible for the sake of whatever we most value and cherish — better health, higher living standards, a greater sense of family and community, profitable progress, inner richness and more regard for the whole planet. We can have them all.

See into your own heart, into the heart of your organization and into the heart of creativity itself. See for yourself the potential that lies there.

This program is dedicated to a world beyond scarcity and separation, to a world where each person prospers materially and spiritually.

Ultimately, the value of this program is not what it says, but what people like you do with the thoughts and information it contains. What you will do is your gift to us.

Thank You.

"We went to the moon as technicians; we returned as humanitarians."

■ Edgar Mitchell

Our Special Thanks To:

Janice Van Collie for her great ability to create an architecture for this program, and for her special commitment to taking this journey together.

Diane Dias for her creative book design, and David Page and Barbara McGregor for their wonderful, artistic illustrations.

Dale Gardner, Roger James, Joy Watson, Karen Wilhelm Buckley, and Tomi Nagai-Rothe for their constructive review of the workbook manuscript.

Joe McPherson for bringing me into the field of creativity and innovation.

Joy Watson for her moral support and her insights into the structure of "Mind Fitness™."

Lorna Catford and Cathy DeForest for their special contributions to the "journey" model of the creative process.

To Sharon Jeffrey for providing insights into the use of values in the workplace.

Jagdish Parikh and the International Management Institute for their pioneering research on the application of intuition in business.

Sue McKibbon, Rae Levine, Nancy Madigan, and Vic Ortiz for their active support.

All our other friends, our clients and the families of the project team whose encouragement and cooperation help make this project possible.

Global Creativity Corporation

Our mission at Global Creativity Corporation is to develop and inspire leaders to encourage innovation, expand intelligence, and exercise integrity in order to make a purposeful difference in the world.

For more information about the Global Creativity Corporation, please visit or contact them on the web:

WEB: www.globalcreativity.com
EMAIL CONTACT: wmiller@globalcreativity.com